# DEADLY IMPASSE

What ails the Indo-Pakistani relationship? Rivalry between the two states has persisted since the partition of the British Indian Empire in 1947 and despite negotiations, four wars and multiple crises, India and Pakistan remain locked in a long-standing dispute. Evaluating relations from 1999 through to 2009, Sumit Ganguly seeks to understand this troubled relationship and why efforts at peace-making and conflict resolution, which have included unilateral Indian concessions, have not been more fruitful. Charting key sources of tension throughout the decade, including the origins and outcomes of the Kargil War in 1999, developments in the Indian-controlled portion of the state of Kashmir, the attack on the Indian parliament in December 2001 and the onset of the 2001–2 crisis, *Deadly Impasse* sets out to discover whether the roots of this hostile relationship stem from security dilemmas or reflect the dynamics between a status quo power and a predatory state.

SUMIT GANGULY is a professor of political science and holds the Rabindranath Tagore Chair in Indian Cultures and Civilizations at Indiana University, Bloomington.

# Deadly Impasse

## Kashmir and Indo-Pakistani Relations at the Dawn of a New Century

SUMIT GANGULY

*Indiana University, Bloomington*

# CAMBRIDGE
## UNIVERSITY PRESS

University Printing House, Cambridge CB2 8BS, United Kingdom

One Liberty Plaza, 20th Floor, New York, NY 10006, USA

477 Williamstown Road, Port Melbourne, VIC 3207, Australia

314-321, 3rd Floor, Plot 3, Splendor Forum, Jasola District Centre, New Delhi - 110025, India

103 Penang Road, #05-06/07, Visioncrest Commercial, Singapore 238467

Cambridge University Press is part of the University of Cambridge.

It furthers the University's mission by disseminating knowledge in the pursuit of education, learning and research at the highest international levels of excellence.

www.cambridge.org
Information on this title: www.cambridge.org/9780521125680

© Sumit Ganguly 2016

First published 2016

*A catalogue record for this publication is available from the British Library*

ISBN 978-0-521-76361-5 Hardback
ISBN 978-0-521-12568-0 Paperback

Cambridge University Press has no responsibility for the persistence or accuracy of URLs for external or third-party internet websites referred to in this publication, and does not guarantee that any content on such websites is, or will remain, accurate or appropriate.

*To Traci*

# CONTENTS

# MAPS

# PREFACE AND ACKNOWLEDGMENTS

This manuscript has had a long gestation period. The original idea stemmed from a plan to update my previous book, *The Crisis in Kashmir: Portents of War, Hopes of Peace*. However, my imaginative and supportive editor at Cambridge University Press, Edward Parsons, upon reading my proposal suggested that I write a wholly new book. His generous suggestion led to the genesis of this book. It does not merely seek to update developments in Kashmir but instead attempts to probe what ails the Indo-Pakistani relationship and prevents a resolution of the long-standing dispute. It argues that the two parties are not on an equal footing; Pakistan is the revisionist state in this relationship and India is the status quo power. This argument is not a normative statement; instead it is merely the description of an empirical reality.

I am deeply grateful to a number of individuals who have read and commented on the manuscript. My most able, thoughtful and generous critics are two former doctoral students, Nicolas Blarel and Manjeet Pardesi. Both of them read the manuscript with care, proffered important theoretical and substantive suggestions and forced me to clarify my arguments in various places. Colonel David O. Smith, a friend of many years, who served twice as the United States Defense Attaché in Islamabad, Pakistan, also provided timely, thoughtful and trenchant comments on this manuscript. Professor Robert Jervis, who has long been a staunch intellectual supporter, read the manuscript with much care and provided me with extensive and perspicacious comments. Finally, I wish to thank an anonymous reviewer for Cambridge University Press who provided critical, but entirely helpful, suggestions for improving the manuscript. The usual caveats apply.

I also wish to thank the following individuals for their assistance. My research assistant, Brandon Miliate, proofread this manuscript with care, pitched in as needed to track down errant endnotes, and created the bibliography and appendices. Karen Stoll Farrell, the Librarian for South and Southeast Asia at the Wells Library and Indiana University, Bloomington helped locate relevant documents in a most timely fashion. Her colleague, Theresa Quill, the Social Sciences and GIS Librarian, worked closely and attentively with me to create the accompanying maps. Jack Renner, an intern at the Center on American and Global Security at Indiana University Bloomington, carefully constructed the economic data charts.

Finally, I would be remiss if I did not thank my previous editor at Cambridge University Press, Marigold Acland, and my current editor, Lucy Rhymer, for their generous encouragement, extraordinary patience and unstinted support.

# ABBREVIATIONS

| | |
|---|---|
| CBM | Confidence Building Measure |
| CCS | Cabinet Committee on Security |
| CFL | Ceasefire Line |
| HuM | Hizb-ul-Mujahideen |
| IAF | Indian Air Force |
| ISAF | International Security Assistance Force |
| ISI-D | Inter-Services Intelligence Directorate |
| JeM | Jaish-e-Mohammed |
| LeT | Lashkar-e-Taiba |
| LoC | Line of Control |
| NAM | Non-Aligned Movement |
| NIA | National Investigation Agency |
| NLI | Northern Light Infantry |
| PAF | Pakistan Air Force |
| PLA | People's Liberation Army |
| PPP | Pakistan People's Party |
| PRC | People's Republic of China |
| SAARC | South Asian Association for Regional Cooperation |

# I

# The rivalry revisited

## THE SOURCES OF DISCORD

What animates the Indo-Pakistani conflict? The question is far from trivial. This rivalry, which originated almost immediately after British colonial withdrawal from and the partition of the British Indian Empire in 1947, has proven to be remarkably durable.[1] It has resulted in four wars (1947–48, 1965, 1971 and 1999) and multiple crises.[2] The structural origins of this conflict have been explored at length elsewhere.[3]

This book, focused on Indo-Pakistani relations between 1999 and 2009, will attempt to answer a critical question: does the *security dilemma* (the *spiral model*) or the *deterrence model* best describe this relationship?[4] This attempt to squarely place the rivalry in the

---

1 For a particularly thoughtful account of the process of partition and the drawing of the Indo-Pakistani border see Lucy P. Chester, *Borders and Conflict in South Asia: The Radcliffe Boundary Commission and the Partition of the Punjab* (Manchester: Manchester University Press, 2009).

2 Sumit Ganguly, *Conflict Unending: India-Pakistan Tensions Since 1947* (New York: Columbia University Press, 2001).

3 For an Indian perspective on the British transfer of power see V.P. Menon, *The Transfer of Power in India* (New Delhi: Orient Blackswan, 1997); for a Pakistani perspective see Chaudhry Mohammed Ali, *The Emergence of Pakistan* (Lahore: Research Society of Pakistan, 1983).

4 For a clear discussion of these two models see Robert Jervis, *Perception and Misperception in International Politics* (Princeton: Princeton University Press, 1976), p. 81.

context of central propositions from the security studies literature is a fundamentally novel endeavor.

The novelty of this approach is twofold. First, despite the persistence of this rivalry over six decades, the literature on the subject is scant.[5] What little does exists is either descriptive or historical in orientation and there have been few attempts to examine the rivalry through theoretical foci.[6] Second, this lack of scholarly attention to the sources of discord is puzzling, as the two states have been incipient nuclear-armed rivals for well over two decades and became overt nuclear weapons states in 1998. Furthermore, one of the two rivals, India, has long had aspirations to emerge as a great power. Indeed, according to some scholars, it has already achieved great power status.[7]

Some recent literature, mostly focused on Pakistan, while not explicitly alluding to the concept of the *security dilemma*, has nevertheless suggested that the sheer structural differences between the two states at the time of their emergence from the detritus of the British colonial empire in South Asia, led the weaker state, Pakistan, to fear its behemoth neighbor. To varying degrees, these works suggest that misgivings about India precipitated Pakistan's anxieties and set the stage for the rivalry.[8] Before turning to a discussion of

---

5  See for example Jyoti Bhusan Das Gupta, *Indo-Pakistan Relations, 1947–1955* (Amsterdam: De Brug Djambatan, 1958); Sisir Gupta, *Kashmir: A Study in India-Pakistan Relations* (New Delhi: Asia Publishing House, 1967); Russell Brines, *The Indo-Pakistani Conflict* (New York: Pall Mall, 1968).

6  For an attempt at theorizing about the conflict see T.V. Paul (ed.), *The Indo-Pakistani Conflict: An Enduring Rivalry* (New York: Cambridge University Press, 2006); for a critique thereof see Sumit Ganguly, "War, Nuclear Weapons and Crisis Stability in South Asia," *Security Studies* 17, no. 1 (2008): 164–184.

7  Manjeet S. Pardesi, "Is India a Great Power? Understanding Great Power Status in Contemporary International Relations," *Asian Security* 11, no. 1 (2015): 1–30.

8  See for example, Ayesha Jalal, *The Struggle for Pakistan: A Muslim Homeland and Global Politics* (Cambridge, MA: Harvard University Press, 2014); also see Aqil Shah, *The Army and Democracy: Military Politics in Pakistan* (Cambridge, MA: Harvard University Press, 2014). It should be noted that Shah's argument, in some significant degree, differs from that of Jalal. Whereas Jalal suggests that India's size and initial intransigence set off Pakistan's fears, Shah argues that the Pakistani military establishment helped stoke those fears for its own parochial interests. An important exception to these analyses, and whose argument comports with mine, is C. Christine Fair, *Fighting to the End: The Pakistan Army's Way of War* (New York: Oxford University Press, 2014); Fair's argument

the *security dilemma* and *deterrence models* and their applicability to the Indo-Pakistani conflict it appears necessary to provide a brief account of the evolution of the rivalry.

The rivalry, from the outset, became structured within the territorial dispute over the state of Jammu and Kashmir. Briefly stated, the problem of the Kashmir dispute can be traced to the process of British colonial disengagement from the subcontinent. At the time of independence and partition there were two classes of states in British India. These were the states of British India and the so-called princely states. The latter had enjoyed nominal independence as long as they recognized the British Crown as the paramount power in South Asia and deferred to the British on matters of defense, foreign affairs and communications. Lord Mountbatten, the last Viceroy, had decreed that the princely states had to join either India or Pakistan based upon their demographic composition and their geographic location.[9] Kashmir posed a unique problem because it was a Muslim-majority state but with a Hindu monarch and abutted both India and Pakistan.[10] In the

is that Pakistan is not a security seeking state but a "greedy state." She traces the roots of Pakistan's behavior to its national ideology.

9   It is necessary at this juncture to state quite forthrightly that a controversy exists about the drawing of the borders at the time of independence and partition. A noted British historian, Alastair Lamb, has alleged that Lord Mountbatten influenced Sir Cyril Radcliffe, the London barrister who was entrusted with the task of delineating the boundaries of the two nascent states in drawing the partition line to ensure that a portion of Kashmir actually touched India. Lamb's allegation holds that the territory ceded to India was not a Muslim-majority region and therefore should not have been granted to India. Furthermore, Lamb claims that the Instrument of Accession, under the aegis of which Kashmir went to India, was signed after Indian troops had already landed in Srinagar. The first claim, on the basis of a careful examination of the demographic features of the border at the time of independence, can actually be refuted. The second remains a matter of debate and conjecture. For the purposes of this analysis the critical issue of the fairness of the drawing of the borders is deemed uncontroversial.For a response to Lamb, see Prem Shankar Jha, *Kashmir 1947: Rival Versions of History* (New Delhi: Oxford University Press, 2003).

10  For the origins of the controversy see Alastair Lamb, *Kashmir: A Disputed Legacy* (Hertingfordbury: Roxford Books, 1991). For a superb rejoinder to Lamb based upon a careful sifting of demographic data see Shereen Ilahi, "The Radcliffe Boundary Commission and the Fate of Kashmir," *India Review* 2, no. 1 (January 2003): 77–102.

event, Maharaja Hari Singh, the monarch of Kashmir, chose not to accede to either state.[11]

As Hari Singh vacillated, Pakistan embarked upon a military strategy to wrest the state from India. It involved sending in Pakistani troops disguised as and mingled with local tribesmen to help foment a revolt against Hari Singh's rule.[12] As the Pakistan-aided rebels advanced toward Srinagar, the summer capital of his state, Maharaja Hari Singh, in panic, appealed to India for assistance. Prime Minister Nehru agreed to provide assistance but only if two conditions were met. The maharaja would have to accede to India and in the absence of a referendum to ascertain the wishes of the Kashmiri population, Sheikh Mohammed Abdullah, the leader of the principal, secular, popular party within the state would have to grant his imprimatur to the process.[13] Only when Abdullah gave his consent did Nehru permit Indian military forces to be flown into the state to stop the Pakistani-assisted tribal advance.[14]

The Indian military contingent managed to stop the Pakistani military onslaught but not before one-third of the state fell to the invaders.[15] On the advice of Lord Mountbatten the case was referred

11  His reasons were fairly straightforward. He did not wish to join Pakistan because as the ruler of a Muslim-majority state, who was not known for his benevolence toward his Muslim subjects, he feared that he would not fare well in a state that had been created as the homeland for the Muslims of South Asia. He also did not wish to join India because he knew that a socialist-leaning prime minister, Nehru, would strip him of most of his vast privileges. His fears, thereby, were hardly unfounded. For details see Jyoti Bhusan Das Gupta, *Jammu and Kashmir* (The Hague: Martinus Nijhoff, 1968); the obverse of this problem, up to a point, obtained in the princely state of Hyderabad where the Nizam, a Muslim ruler, presided over a Hindu-majority population. The difference, of course, lay in that Hyderabad did not share a border with Pakistan and was completely landlocked.

12  The particulars of Pakistan's military strategy can be found in Akbar Khan, *Raiders in Kashmir* (Lahore: National Book Foundation, 1975).

13  On Abdullah's imprimatur see Leo E. Rose and Richard Sisson, *War and Secession: Pakistan, India, and the Creation of Bangladesh* (Oakland: University of California Press, 1991); on Abdullah's popularity in the state see Ian Copeland, "The Abdullah Factor: Kashmiri Muslims and the Crisis of 1947," in D.A. Low (ed.), *The Political Inheritance of Pakistan* (New York: St. Martin's Press, 1991).

14  Lionel Protip Sen, *Slender Was the Thread* (New Delhi: Orient Longmans, 1969).

15  The most dispassionate account of the Pakistani invasion and India's response can be found in Andrew Whitehead, *A Mission in Kashmir* (New York: Penguin, 2008).

to the United Nations on January 1, 1948 under the aegis of Chapter Seven of the United Nations Charter, which deals with matters pertaining to breaches of international peace and security. Following much discussion and the passage of multiple resolutions, the United Nations called for a ceasefire on January 1, 1949. This ceasefire was codified in the creation of a Ceasefire Line (CFL) that reflected the disposition of troops at the time.[16]

Subsequently, the issue quickly became embroiled in the politics of the Cold War. The Western powers, most notably the United Kingdom and subsequently the United States, did not deal dispassionately with the subject but instead allowed their geopolitical interests in Pakistan to shape their policies.[17] Nevertheless, the United Nations did pass two critical resolutions, which enjoined Pakistan to withdraw its troops, asked India to create conditions conducive to holding a plebiscite and then to conduct a plebiscite to determine the wishes of the Kashmiri population. As is well known, Pakistan refused to comply with the initial step and India, in turn, failed to follow through on the subsequent expectations. The matter followed a desultory course in the United Nations for almost two decades. Eventually, in the 1960s the UN lost interest in the subject.

In the aftermath of the disastrous Sino-Indian border war of 1962, India desperately sought military assistance from both the United States and the United Kingdom. Aware of India's strategic vulnerability, the two powers played a critical role in inducing bilateral discussions between India and Pakistan. These discussions stemmed from the Harriman/Sandys Mission, which had brought Averell Harriman, a US Assistant Secretary of State, and Duncan Sandys, a British Member of Parliament and Commonwealth Secretary to India. They successfully persuaded Prime Minister Nehru to hold talks with Pakistan with a view toward seeking a resolution of the Kashmir dispute. Faced with a looming military threat from the People's Republic of China (PRC) and dependent on both diplomatic and military support from both powers, Nehru had reluctantly agreed to hold talks. Between December 1962 and May 1963 a set of bilateral talks were held in a number of different locations

---

16 For details see Ganguly, 2001, pp. 16–19.
17 Chandrasekhar Dasgupta, *War and Diplomacy in Kashmir, 1947–1948* (New Delhi: Sage, 2002).

in India and Pakistan. Despite much Anglo-American pressure on India to reach an accord favorable to Pakistan, Nehru's otherwise beleaguered regime refused to give ground.[18]

Indeed the failure of multilateral negotiations and these bilateral talks played vital roles in precipitating the second Indo-Pakistani conflict in 1965.[19] This war ended in a military stalemate. Following its outbreak the United States imposed an arms embargo on both states irritating both parties in the process. The impact on Pakistan, however, was considerably greater as the vast majority of its equipment was of American origin. In the aftermath of the war, the United States evinced little interest in the problem. The Soviet Union, sensing an opportunity to expand its influence in South Asia, stepped into the breach. To that end it invited Nehru's successor, Prime Minister Shastri and President Ayub Khan, to the Central Asian city of Tashkent to broker a postwar accord. Under the terms of the Tashkent Agreement the two sides agreed to return to the *status quo ante* and to abjure from the use of force to settle the Kashmir dispute.

A third war took place between India and Pakistan in 1971. This conflict, however, did not have its origins in the Kashmir dispute. Instead it can be traced to the exigencies of Pakistani domestic politics. In the wake of Pakistan's first free and fair election in December 1970, the Awami League, an East Pakistan-based political party led by Sheikh Mujibur Rehman, won an overwhelming victory in the province. In West Pakistan, the Pakistan People's Party (PPP) swept the polls. Given this bifurcated electoral verdict the two sides needed to reach a power-sharing agreement. As negotiations ensued it became increasingly apparent that the PPP (and its military backers) had little or no interest in arriving at an accord that would involve a genuinely equitable arrangement.[20] Indeed by March 1971 the two parties found themselves in a virtual deadlock. Of course, the military, which had little or

---

18  For details see Rudra Chaudhuri, *Forged in Crisis: India and the United States Since 1947* (London: Christopher Hurst and Company, 2014), pp. 126–148.

19  On the origins of the 1965 war see Sumit Ganguly, "Deterrence Failure Revisited: The Indo-Pakistani Conflict of 1965," *Journal of Strategic Studies* 13, no. 4 (December 1990): 77–93.

20  Rounaq Jahan, *Pakistan: Failure in National Integration* (New York: Columbia University Press, 1972).

no interest whatsoever in any power-sharing arrangement, abandoned the negotiations at the behest of the president and a coterie of senior generals.[21]

Meanwhile, the supporters of the Awami League in East Pakistan ramped up their demands and sought to extract an unprecedented degree of autonomy from the West. Their stance was hardly unreasonable given that since independence the West had, for all practical purposes, dominated the politics and economics of the country.[22]

As the impasse persisted, the Pakistani military embarked on a crackdown on East Pakistan's attentive public on March 26, 1971, especially in the capital city of Dacca (now Dhaka). Over the course of the week the Pakistan Army killed over one hundred thousand civilians.[23] Faced with this repression several million East Pakistanis fled the country and sought refuge in various Indian border states. By May of 1971, the refugee influx had reached nearly ten million.[24]

Faced with this refugee burden, India's policy-makers quickly concluded that they could ill-afford to absorb them into India's already turgid population. Though they went through the motions of seeking a diplomatic solution to the ongoing crisis, they started to formulate a contingency plan for the invasion of East Pakistan designed to break off the province from the West. Over the course of the next several months, even as some diplomatic activity ensued, India's security forces and intelligence services started to train, equip and support an indigenous Bengali insurgency movement, the Mukti Bahini (literally "liberation force"). Pakistani authorities protested India's covert involvement in the politics of East Pakistan but India's support did not flag. Unable to quell the internal rebellion, which was gathering steam thanks to India's efforts, the Pakistani Air Force struck at India's northern bases on December 6, 1971. This attack, which proved to be mostly

---

21 On this point, which challenges the conventional wisdom that the talks had broken down, see Jalal, 2014, p. 172.
22 Rose and Sisson, 1991.
23 The best treatment of this tragedy can be found in Gary J. Bass, *The Blood Telegram: Nixon, Kissinger and a Forgotten Genocide* (New York: Knopf, 2013).
24 Robert Jackson, *South Asian Crisis: India, Pakistan, Bangla Desh* (London: Chatto & Windus, 1975).

unsuccessful, nevertheless provided India with the formal *casus belli* to invade East Pakistan.[25]

## THE LONG PEACE AND ITS END

After the third Indo-Pakistani conflict in 1971, the region had seen a period of unprecedented, if cold, peace. In considerable part, this long peace in South Asia stemmed from Pakistan's decisive defeat in the 1971 war and the concomitant asymmetry in Indian and Pakistani military capabilities. Furthermore, the Pakistan Army, thanks to the military debacle in East Pakistan, had been mostly discredited, giving a civilian regime some control over the security establishment. Consequently, apart from some tensions in the wake of the Soviet invasion and occupation of Afghanistan when an arms transfer and military nexus was renewed between the United States and Pakistan, the Kashmir issue remained dormant until December 1989.

The only exception was a crisis that took place in 1987. This stemmed from India's attempt to respond to Pakistan's involvement in an indigenous insurgency that was wracking the state of Punjab. The origins of the Punjab insurgency have been discussed at length elsewhere.[26] In the mid-1980s, Pakistan had become deeply embroiled in the insurgency and was providing the insurgents with sanctuary, training and material support.[27] Given that Punjab is located in the Indian heartland, its policy-makers decided that a strong dissuasive message should be sent to Pakistan.

As circumstances would have it, the Indian Army was under the leadership of a flamboyant, US-trained officer, General Krishnaswami Sundarji. General Sundarji was keen on modernizing the Indian military and wanted to pursue a more assertive military doctrine. He was interested in testing an indigenously developed system of radars and telecommunication equipment. To that end, he

---

25 Much of this is discussed in Srinath Raghavan, *1971: A Global History of the Creation of Bangladesh* (Cambridge, MA: Harvard University Press, 2013).

26 On the Punjab insurgency see Gurharpal Singh, *Ethnic Conflict in India: A Case Study of Punjab* (New York: Palgrave Macmillan, 2000).

27 Hamish Telford "Counter-Insurgency in India: Observations from Punjab and Kashmir," *The Journal of Conflict Studies* 21, no. 1 (2001): 1–27.

sought and received permission to carry out a very substantial military exercise, code-named Brasstacks, in the Rajasthan desert bordering Pakistan. The sheer length of the exercise, spanning several months, its extraordinary size, involving close to 150,000 soldiers and its east–west axis provoked Pakistani anxieties.[28] (Most military exercises, in the past, had been held along a north–south axis to avoid conveying any impression that the exercise was a prelude to a possible war.)

Not surprisingly, Pakistan chose not to return some key units to its peacetime stations following the termination of its own winter military exercises "Sledgehammer" and "Flying Horse." Instead, it placed them at some strategic salients along the Indo-Pakistani border. These Pakistani military moves, in turn, led to serious misgivings in New Delhi and generated fears of a possible war. Such fears were not entirely unfounded, given the deeply disturbed situation within the Punjab and the links between some of the Punjabi separatist groups and Pakistan's intelligence agencies. As tensions mounted, US and Soviet diplomats (and intelligence specialists), who had followed the emergence of this spiral, used their good offices to intercede in both Islamabad and New Delhi in attempts to defuse the situation.

As the crisis drew to a close, one of the principal architects of Pakistan's nuclear weapons program, Abdul Qadir Khan, gave an interview to a noted Indian journalist, Kuldip Nayar, in which he asserted that Pakistan was well within reach of fashioning a nuclear weapon. It is not wholly clear if Khan's revelation constituted a deliberate attempt at nuclear signaling. However, Indian authorities did take this disclosure seriously and boosted their own covert nuclear weapons program.[29] Though the crisis did not escalate into a war thanks to timely superpower intercession, it reinforced in New Delhi existing misgivings about Pakistani military regimes and of General Zia-ul-Haq, the Pakistani military dictator, in particular.

---

28  Steven R. Weisman, "On India's Border, A Huge Mock War," *New York Times*, March 6, 1987.
29  Much of this discussion about the Brasstacks crisis has been derived from Kanti Bajpai, P.R. Chari, Pervaiz Iqbal Cheema, Stephen P. Cohen and Sumit Ganguly, *Brasstacks and Beyond: Perception and the Management of Crisis in South Asia* (New Delhi: Manohar Books, 1995).

General Zia, of course, perished in a mysterious plane crash in the summer of 1988. His abrupt death led the Pakistani military to return to the barracks. Their decision not to cling on to power stemmed from US pressures as well as a realization that the populace had tired of military rule. Benazir Bhutto, the daughter of the Pakistani president, Zulfikar Ali Bhutto, who General Zia had sent to the gallows, assumed office in an election that was deemed to be free and fair. Shortly thereafter she evinced a willingness to start discussions with India to try and improve relations. These efforts, quite apart from the ingrained hostility of the security establishment, quickly proved to be abortive.

In December 1989, an indigenous, ethno-religious insurgency erupted in the Indian-controlled portion of the disputed state of Jammu and Kashmir. The internal dimensions of this crisis, like that in the Punjab, also stemmed primarily from various shortcomings in India's federal order. The incipient peace process that Bhutto, along with her Indian counterpart, Prime Minister Rajiv Gandhi, had initiated was now placed in jeopardy.[30] The abrupt onset of the rebellion in Indian-controlled Kashmir effectively ended these nascent discussions.

Shortly thereafter the insurgency threatened to spin out of control as Indian authorities proved wholly incapable of coping with it. Within the year of the outbreak of the insurgency, Pakistan's Inter-Services Intelligence Directorate (ISI-D) worked assiduously to transform it from a grassroots uprising into a well-orchestrated, religiously inspired and externally supported extortion racket.[31] The Indian state initially responded in a ham-fisted fashion to quell the insurgents. Its initial approach was to use extensive force against the insurgents. Ironically, this strategy produced perverse results. It had the effect of further inflaming the sentiments of the local population and widened the scope of the insurgency.

30 On the origins of the insurgency see Sumit Ganguly, *The Crisis in Kashmir: Portents of War, Hopes of Peace* (New York: Cambridge University Press, 1997).
31 For the role of the ISI-D see Arif Jamal, *Shadow War: The Untold Story of Jihad in Kashmir* (New York: Melville House, 2009) and Praveen Swami, *India, Pakistan and the Secret Jihad: The Covert War in Kashmir, 1947–2004* (London: Routledge, 2007).

Indeed in 1990 India quickly found itself embroiled in yet another crisis with Pakistan. This crisis had its origins in India's inability to restore a modicum of order to the Kashmir valley, the principal locus of the insurgency. As Indian authorities sought to contain the insurgency they warned Pakistan that continued infiltration into Kashmir could lead to a conflict with India. Pakistani authorities, in turn, turned up their rhetoric threatening a war with India. In the United States, intelligence officials warned that the escalating rhetoric (as well as some critical troop movements) made the situation in the subcontinent quite fraught, with the possibility of an inadvertent conflict. In May 1990, the then deputy National Security Adviser, Robert Gates, accompanied by Richard Haas, the Senior Director for South Asia and the Middle East on the United States National Security Council, traveled to both New Delhi and Islamabad in an attempt to defuse the crisis. In New Delhi, Gates counseled restraint on India. In Islamabad he delivered a different message. Not only did he suggest that the Pakistanis end their support for the insurgents but also warned that in every war game scenario that the United States had developed, Pakistan emerged as the loser.[32] Though Pakistani infiltration did not come to an end, the crisis was effectively defused.

On the Indian side, faced with widespread domestic and external criticism of its harsh methods, New Delhi changed its tactics and within a few years managed to restore a modicum of order, if not law, in the state.[33] Meanwhile, despite changes in regime within Pakistan, the fundamental commitment to the use of proxy terrorist forces in Kashmir continued apace, thereby keeping relations with India on the boil.

Against this backdrop of ongoing tensions, considerable international concern was focused on the subcontinent in the wake of

---

32 For details see Devin T. Hagerty, "Nuclear Deterrence in South Asia: The 1990 Indo-Pakistani Crisis," *International Security* 20, no. 3 (Winter 1995): 79–114; also see Sumit Ganguly and Devin Hagerty, *Fearful Symmetry: India-Pakistan Crises Under the Shadow of Nuclear Weapons* (Seattle: University of Washington Press, 2006); and P.R. Chari, Pervaiz Iqbal Cheema and Stephen P. Cohen, *Perception, Politics and Security in South Asia: The Compound Crisis of 1990* (London: RoutledgeCurzon, 2003).

33 On the evolution of India's Counter-insurgency tactics see Sumit Ganguly and David P. Fidler (eds.), *India and Counterinsurgency: Lessons Learned* (London: Routledge, 2009).

the Indian and Pakistani nuclear tests of May 1998.[34] The United States, along with much of the international community, expressed considerable dismay and anger over the nuclear tests.[35] Not surprisingly, both sides faced a raft of bilateral and multilateral sanctions. The United States, in particular, mounted a major diplomatic effort to try and persuade both states to roll back their nuclear weapons programs. In the end, however, this proved to be a futile endeavor.

Their mutual and overt acquisition of nuclear weapons in 1998 deepened a debate, which had begun in the late 1980s, about whether or not the region is more or less likely to witness full-scale conflict. Some have argued that the nuclear deterrence may well prevent the outbreak of a major conflict. Others argue that the possibility of war is greater because Pakistan, a revisionist state, believes that it can now provoke India, a status quo power, with impunity, because of its nuclear shield. In fact, the fourth Indo-Pakistani conflict in 1999 in the region of Kargil only helped sharpen the contours of the debate. Those who argued the case for "strategic pessimism" believed that escalation had been narrowly averted through a set of idiosyncratic circumstances. On the other hand, those who believed in the robustness of nuclear deterrence held that full-scale war did not ensue precisely because of the mutual possession of nuclear weapons.[36]

This debate has yet to yield a clear-cut answer. However, before one seeks a definitive answer to that question it may be useful to ascertain what underlying factors drive this relationship of hostility. Can the sources of hostility be traced simply to structural conditions? Namely, is this relationship merely a *security dilemma*?[37]

---

34  On the origins of the nuclear tests see Sumit Ganguly, "India's Pathway to Pokhran II: The Sources and Prospects of India's Nuclear Weapons Program," *International Security* 23, no. 4 (Spring 1999): 148–177; on Pakistan's motivations see Samina Ahmed, "Pakistan's Nuclear Weapons Program: Turning Points and Nuclear Choices," *International Security* 23, no. 4 (Spring 1999): 178–204.

35  A good account of the US response can be gleaned from Strobe Talbott, *Democracy, Diplomacy and the Bomb* (Washington, DC: The Brookings Institution, 2006).

36  Sumit Ganguly and S. Paul Kapur, *India, Pakistan and the Bomb: Debating Nuclear Stability in South Asia* (New York: Columbia University Press, 2010).

37  For the classic statement of the concept of the *security dilemma* see John H. Herz, "Idealist Internationalism and the Security Dilemma, *World Politics* 2, no. 2 (January 1950): 157–180; for re-statements and refinements see

Pared to the bone, this concept holds that in an anarchic international system a state cannot be certain that another's acquisition of military capabilities is purely defensive. Since intentions can change, the same weaponry can be used for offensive purposes. Consequently, a state must respond to the other's choices. In turn, its decisions provoke the anxieties of the other, thereby contributing to a spiral of hostility.

On the other hand, the security dilemma may explain little when one state is not reconciled to the status quo but actually wishes to bring about territorial changes. Under these circumstances one party amounts to a revisionist state and the other might be considered a status quo power. Consequently, steps that the status quo power undertakes to assuage the apparent misgivings of the revisionist power may accomplish little. On the contrary, such conciliatory gestures may actually be construed as signs of weakness and embolden the revisionist state. Furthermore, in the Indo-Pakistani case, psychological dynamics affecting decision-making have repeatedly skewed Pakistani assessments of Indian capability and resolve. These have involved various cognitive and affective biases leading to questionable and contradictory evaluations of India's will and capability.[38]

Given Pakistan's relentless efforts to alter the territorial status quo it needs to be carefully underscored that the central argument of this book is that it is indeed a revisionist power. It is not, as several scholars have argued, fears of Indian malfeasance that drive Pakistan's insecurities. Specific events and choices, on particular occasions, may have provoked Pakistani concerns. However, there is little or no question that Pakistan remains unalterably committed to changing the territorial status quo regardless of Indian behavior.

COMPETING AND ANTAGONISTIC NATIONAL VISIONS

What explains the apparently unyielding positions of the two antagonists to the Kashmir dispute? Suffice to say that it is rooted

Robert Jervis, "Cooperation Under the Security Dilemma," *World Politics* 30, no. 2 (January 1976): 167–214; also see Ken Booth and Nicholas Wheeler (eds.), *The Security Dilemma: Fear, Cooperation and Trust in World Politics* (New York: Palgrave Macmillan, 2007).

38 On this subject see Ganguly, 1990; also see Altaf Gauhar, "Four Wars, One Assumption," *The Nation*, September 5, 1999.

in competing visions of state construction in South Asia. India, which was based upon the principle of secular, civic nationalism, finds itself at odds with Pakistan, which was founded on the basis of religious nationalism.[39]

Any discussion of the Indo-Pakistani discord must take into account certain structural differences between the two polities. Shortly after the partition of the British Indian Empire and the creation of the independent states of India and Pakistan, the political trajectories of the two states diverged dramatically. Within three years of its independence, India managed to forge a secular and democratic constitution and succeeded in holding national elections two years thereafter.[40] Pakistan, on the other hand, failed to draft a constitution until nine years after its independence. Jinnah's early demise in 1948 and the assassination of his handpicked successor, Liaquat Ali Khan, in 1951 further deteriorated the situation. The absence of these two key individuals in the country's nascent political order certainly did little to help the process of political and ideological consolidation. Following a period of political turmoil this constitutional experiment drew to a close in 1958 with the first military coup.[41] Military rule in Pakistan would then last until 1969. Indeed the vast majority of Pakistan's independent history the country has been under authoritarian military rule.[42]

The origins of the different political pathways of these two states have been discussed elsewhere. Suffice it to state that they can be traced to the ideology, organization and political strategies of the two nationalist movements.[43] The Indian nationalist movement, despite its elitist origins, managed under the leadership of Mohandas Gandhi

39  On Pakistani nationalism see Hafeez Malik, *Muslim Nationalism in India and Pakistan* (Washington, DC: Public Affairs Press, 1963); on the origins of Indian nationalism see Ramachandra Guha, *India After Gandhi: The History of the World's Largest Democracy* (New York: Ecco, 2007); also see Jawaharlal Nehru, *The Discovery of India* (New Delhi: Oxford University Press, 1994).

40  Granville Austin, *The Indian Constitution: Cornerstone of a Nation* (New Delhi: Oxford University Press, 1999).

41  Allen McGrath, *The Destruction of Pakistan's Democracy* (Karachi: Oxford University Press, 1996).

42  Sumit Ganguly, "Pakistan's Never-Ending Story: Why the October Coup Was No Surprise, *Foreign Affairs* 79, no. 2 (March/April 2000): 2–9.

43  See the excellent treatment in Maya Tudor, *The Promise of Power: The Origins of Authoritarianism in Pakistan and Democracy in India* (Cambridge: Cambridge University Press, 2013).

to develop a mass political base in the 1930s, succeeded in promoting internal democracy, allowed internal debate within its ranks and fashioned a blueprint for governance long before independence.

The Pakistani nationalist movement, however, failed to promote internal democracy, remained woven around the charismatic personality of Muhammad Ali Jinnah and drew its support primarily from the landed gentry of the United Provinces (later Uttar Pradesh in independent India) of British India. Furthermore, it should be underscored that Jinnah, unlike his Indian counterpart, Jawaharlal Nehru, who sought electoral legitimacy, chose to govern the Pakistani polity as an unelected Governor-General. Additionally, some authoritarian tendencies emerged in the early days of the Pakistani polity. Almost immediately after independence, Jinnah had dismissed a non-League government in the North West Frontier Province on the most tenuous legal grounds.[44] Finally, as early as 1951, Pakistan faced its first coup attempt in what came to be known as the Rawalpindi Conspiracy Case.[45]

Indian nationalists, shortly after independence, were able to draw of their past background of debate, discussion and argument to quickly fashion a working democratic polity.[46] Their Pakistani counterparts, on the contrary, found themselves overwhelmed with the tasks of state construction, the maintenance of political order, and felt compelled to turn to the military to quell civil disturbances. They also quickly became bogged down in the question of the role of Islam in public life. That issue, of course, still has not been resolved and continues to dog the Pakistani polity.

The emergent internal political arrangements of the two states also produced markedly different patterns of civil–military relations. In Pakistan, the military quickly emerged as *primus inter pares*.[47] Long after the restoration of democracy, albeit for varying lengths of time, democratic civilian authority has not been consolidated in

44 Khalid bin Sayeed, *Pakistan: The Formative Phase, 1947–1948* (Karachi: Pakistan Publishing House, 1960).

45 Hasan Zaheer, *The Rawalpindi Conspiracy 1951: The First Coup Attempt in Pakistan* (Karachi: Oxford University Press, 1998).

46 The best statement of these two contrasting nationalist movements can be found in Paul R. Brass, *Language, Religion and Politics in North India* (Cambridge: Cambridge University Press, 1974).

47 Sayeed, 1960.

the country.[48] The military dominance of the Pakistani polity quite early in the day led to a fundamental distortion of the state's social and economic priorities. According to a knowledgeable source, even before the first coup, the military had managed to divert as much as 70 percent of all government expenditures to meeting national security objectives.[49] That said, India did have the distinct advantage of inheriting most of the military infrastructure of British India.

The military in India, in marked contrast, has been quite subservient to political authority.[50] Even during the brief state of emergency in the late 1970s when Prime Minister Indira Gandhi suspended civil liberties, the military played no role in the political affairs of the state.[51] On occasion, the highest echelons of the military have expressed particular reservations about policies. However, there is no evidence that they have actually contemplated, let alone plotted, a military takeover.

These differing patterns of politico-military relations have had significant consequences for national security and foreign policy decision-making in the two countries. Apart from a small handful of instances, the Indian military has played little or no role whatsoever in the formulation of India's foreign and security policies. Instead, on a number of occasions, senior military staff have been either reprimanded or entirely removed from their commands because they had, in the eyes of the civilian leadership, breached certain norms of civil–military relations. In Pakistan matters have worked in reverse. The military has challenged, supported and dismissed governments as and when they have deemed necessary. Indeed thanks to their dominance they have made the issue of national security the dominant concern of the Pakistani state.[52] Their conception of national security has involved a form of gross inflation of the putative

48 For the best discussion of civil–military relations in Pakistan see Shah, 2014.

49 Shah, 2014, p. 48.

50 Sumit Ganguly, "From the Defense of the Nation to Aid to the Civil: The Army in Contemporary India," *Journal of Asian and African Affairs* 26 (1991): 1–12; for an idiosyncratic account that takes a contrary view see Srinath Raghavan, "Soldiers, Statesmen, and India's Security Policy," *India Review* 11, no. 2 (April–June 2012): 116–133.

51 On this matter see Stephen P. Cohen, "The Military," in Henry Hart (ed.), *Indira Gandhi's India: A Political System Reappraised* (Boulder: Westview, 1976).

52 T.V. Paul, *The Warrior State: Pakistan in the Contemporary World* (New York: Oxford University Press, 2014).

security threat from India. More to the point, it has been fixated on the disputed status of Kashmir.

Before turning to a theoretical discussion it may be useful to enumerate some general propositions that can be gleaned about the Indo-Pakistani conflict. The first three wars between the two warring states were remarkable for at least six compelling reasons.

First, the common British heritage of the two postcolonial armies profoundly shaped their battle tactics and strategies. Having been trained in the same military establishments prior to independence and partition they relied on World War II, vintage operational plans. Consequently, they used mostly set-piece battle tactics, especially in the 1965 war.[53] Even the highly successful Indian military offensive in the 1971 war in East Pakistan amounted to a "blitzkrieg" strategy derived from the German experience of World War II.[54]

Second, thanks to past professional links it was possible for the higher echelons of the military on both sides to reach informal agreements on the use of force. For example, during the 1965 war, an informal agreement between Air Marshal Asghar Khan of the Pakistani Air Force (PAF) and Air Marshal Arjan Singh of the Indian Air Force (IAF) ensured that population centers in both countries were not bombed at will.[55] It is far from clear that such informal arrangements can be reached in future conflicts. The ties that had once existed amongst senior commanders could not be sustained long after the independence of the two states.

Third, both sides have mostly adhered to the expectations of international law in general and the Geneva Conventions in particular in dealing with their prisoners of war.[56] Even after the 1971 war, despite the seething anger of the ravaged East Pakistani

---

53 Edgar O'Ballance, "The 1965 War in Retrospect," *Defence Journal* 7 (1978): 15–19.

54 John Mearsheimer, *Conventional Deterrence* (Ithaca: Cornell University Press, 1983).

55 See Air-Marshal Asghar Khan, *The First Round: Indo-Pakistan War 1965* (New Delhi: Vikas, 1979).

56 In the wake of the Kargil War of 1999, however, some allegations of torture and summary executions of Indian prisoners of war were reported in the Indian press. The veracity of these claims remains subject to debate. For a

population, India did not permit the mistreatment of Pakistani prisoners of war. Instead 93,000 of them were repatriated to Pakistan after further negotiations following the signing of the Shimla Accord between President Zulfikar Ali Bhutto and Prime Minister Indira Gandhi in 1972.[57]

Fourth, despite the stakes involved, all of these conflicts saw remarkable strategic restraint on the part of both sides. Neither party brought significant amounts of firepower to bear in any of the conflicts. As a consequence, casualties were kept quite limited.[58] Even during the Kargil War of 1999 neither country utilized the considerable firepower that they possessed. Of course, it could be argued that mutual restraint in Kargil could have stemmed from one or a combination of three possible sources. It could be attributed to the mutual possession of nuclear weapons and the concomitant fears of escalation. It could have stemmed from prompt American intervention in this crisis, which sought to tamp down tensions. And finally, it could be traced to the desire of Indian decision-makers to seize the high moral ground and not widen the scope of the conflict.

Fifth, it remains to be seen how future wars will evolve between these two overt, nuclear-armed powers. In the Kargil War, India deliberately circumscribed the scope of the conflict despite significant domestic pressures, the presence of substantial military capabilities and the existence of a jingoistic government. It is, however, a matter of debate if the mutual possession of nuclear weapons had created permissive conditions for the war or whether their existence actually limited the scope of the conflict once it ensued.[59]

Sixth and finally, as at least one scholar has argued, the acquisition of particular military capabilities and the pursuit of specific nuclear postures may render the region more war-prone. This argument challenges the fundamental assumptions of *existential deterrence*, and holds that specific configurations of nuclear forces can

---

detailed accusation see Sunil Nanda, Azhar Abbas, Imtiaz Gul and Ramananda Sengupta, "Raising the Pitch," *Outlook*, June 21, 1999. Available at: www .outlookindia.com/article.aspx?207650.

57  A.G. Noorani, "Search for New Relationships in the Indian Subcontinent," *The World Today* 31, no. 6 (June 1975): 240–248.

58  Ganguly, 2001.    59  Ganguly and Kapur, 2010.

either contribute to greater instability or stability in a particular regional security context.[60]

The origins of the Indo-Pakistani rivalry have been discussed at length elsewhere.[61] This analysis, however, hopes to examine the rivalry using a set of propositions derived from the literature on strategic studies. They are the *deterrence* and *spiral models*.[62] A *deterrence model* would assume that one of the two states involved in an adversarial relationship harbors hostile or malign intentions toward the other and that a war can only be fended off through the adoption of appropriate military strategies that would raise the costs of aggressive behavior. A *spiral model*, however, would argue that the relationship stems from the workings of a *security dilemma*. Accordingly, suitable reassurances on the part of one state should assuage the legitimate security concerns of the other. The concept of the security dilemma has been the subject of much contestation and debate since its inception.[63]

The original concept that had its provenance in the work of Herbert Butterfield was fraught with contradictions, as recent scholarship has demonstrated. Specifically, Butterfield's view of the *security dilemma*, rooted in the flaws of human nature, sat uneasily with the unintended consequences of state behavior. Indeed, as Shiping Tang correctly argues, it was not until John Herz and Robert Jervis sought to build upon the original concept that this issue was forthrightly addressed. Further elaborations and clarifications of this concept have followed and this analysis will rely on two recent such attempts.[64]

60 Vipin Narang, *Nuclear Strategy in the Modern Era: Regional Powers and International Conflict* (Princeton: Princeton University Press, 2014).
61 Ganguly, 2001.
62 For the initial discussion of these two models see Jervis, 1976.
63 For an attempt to refine the concept see Charles L. Glaser, *Rational Theory of International Politics: The Logic of Competition and Cooperation* (Princeton: Princeton University Press, 2010); for an earlier discussion that had highlighted the role of predatory or revisionist states see Randall L. Schweller, "Neorealism's Status-Quo Bias: What Security Dilemma?" *Security Studies* 5, no. 3 (1996): 90–121.
64 Shiping Tang, *A Theory of Security Strategy for Our Time: Defensive Realism* (New York: Palgrave Macmillan, 2010); also see Booth and Wheeler, 2007.

Tang's work, in particular, is of considerable significance as he has attempted to locate the concept in a larger stream of literature of international politics. Key propositions derived from his careful re-formulation of the concept and the theory it is embedded in can be tested in the context of the Indo-Pakistani rivalry. Pared to the bone, Tang argues that the *security dilemma* has three critical components. First, the condition of anarchy contributes to uncertainty, fear and the need for self-help. Second, it requires a lack of malign intentions on the part of either state. Third, and finally, it calls for the accumulation of power (including some offensive capabilities).[65]

Since Tang's work quite specifically stresses the unintentional dimension, we can usefully juxtapose his conception of the *security dilemma* with elements of Charles Glaser's recent work on the same subject.[66] Glaser, both earlier, and in his most recent contribution, has highlighted the existence of what he refers to as "greedy states." Glaser describes them as follows:

A state can also have nonsecurity motives for expansion, which can include the desire to increase its wealth, territory, or prestige, and to spread its political ideology or religion, when these are not required to preserve the state's security. I use the term "greed" to refer to these nonsecurity motives.[67]

Pakistan, this analysis will show, is a "greedy" state. Its desire for expansion does not stem from guaranteeing its own security. Instead it can be traced to its commitment to incorporate the state of Jammu and Kashmir, a piece of territory that its policy-makers (and supporters) believe that India unfairly seized at the time of partition and by virtue of its Muslim-majority status should have been ceded to Pakistan.[68] This irredentist claim to Kashmir has remained a constant in Pakistan's foreign and security policy. What has varied is simply the intensity with which Pakistan's foreign and security policy establishments have pursued this goal. Ironically, it can

---

65 Shiping Tang, "The Security Dilemma: A Conceptual Analysis," *Security Studies* 18, no. 3 (2009): 587–623.

66 For critiques and assessments of Glaser's re-statement see the symposium, Robert Jervis, "Dilemmas about Security Dilemmas," *Security Studies* 20, no. 3 (July-September 2011): 416–489.

67 Glaser, 2010, p. 36.

68 Sir William Barton, "Pakistan's Claim to Kashmir," *Foreign Affairs* 28 (January 1950): 279–308.

be argued that the relentless pursuit of this objective has ill-served Pakistan's own security interests.

What then might be suitable evidence that supports the proposition that Pakistan is not a security-seeking state and what might undermine such an assertion? If Pakistan had been a genuine security-seeking state, and if the *spiral model* was applicable in this context, it would not have initiated the 1947–8 war. At the time of partition and independence the Pakistani state was in considerable institutional disarray and it lacked suitable military resources to make substantial headway against India and yet its leaders chose to undertake the war.[69] One argument holds that the Pakistani leadership initiated the conflict because it feared that India could cut off water supplies to the nascent state as many of the rivers that flow into Pakistan have their origins in the state of Jammu and Kashmir.

However, as at least one Pakistani scholar has shown, Pakistan's successful seizure of a segment of the state in the first war effectively addressed this concern.[70] Having accomplished this critical goal a security-seeking state should have been sated. That, of course, did not prove to be the case. Instead Pakistan again initiated a war with India in an attempt to capture the entire state in 1965.

Further evidence for the *deterrence model* can be derived from the long peace in South Asia between 1972 and 1989. During this time span, thanks to Indian military preponderance and a politically quiescent period in the Indian-controlled segment of the state of Jammu and Kashmir, Pakistan chose not to initiate any conflicts with India. It was only after December 1989, when the indigenous insurgency in the state erupted, that Pakistani policy-makers chose to exploit India's self-inflicted wound. In the absence of the rebellion it is hard to envisage that Pakistan would have chosen to initiate a proxy war against India. Indeed, earlier in the 1980s it had also chosen to exacerbate another insurgency in the Punjab, which also had domestic roots.[71]

69  H.V. Hodson, *The Great Divide: Britain, India and Pakistan* (New York: Random House, 1969).
70  Shah, 2014, p. 40.   71  Telford, 2001.

## ADDRESSING SOME CAVEATS

It is not the purpose of this analysis to pass judgment on the normative basis of Pakistan's claim to Kashmir. Instead Pakistan is seen as a revisionist state simply on the basis that it is intent on re-ordering the territorial arrangements that were reached at the time of British colonial withdrawal from the subcontinent. To Pakistani policy-makers, the status of Kashmir remains the "unfinished business of partition."[72] The roots of this revisionism can be traced to the very ideological basis of the Pakistani state. It was created as the putative homeland of the Muslims of South Asia to escape Hindu domination.[73] Consequently, since Jammu and Kashmir is a Muslim-majority state that abuts Pakistan, it must be merged with Pakistan.

Despite a common religious heritage, East Pakistan broke away (with Indian assistance) from its western counterpart owing to linguistic and economic discrimination.[74] Even Pakistan's break-up in 1971 did not end this claim. In the aftermath of the collapse of the country its policy-makers adopted a different stance to the Kashmir question. In considerable part they arrived at this position because of a realization that they lacked the conventional military means to change the territorial status quo.

Accordingly, they focused their public statements on questions of human rights within Kashmir and the right to Kashmiri self-determination. Pakistan's actions, however, certainly belied both of these claims. First, many of the terrorist organizations that the ISI-D spawned and supported evinced scant, if any regard, for human rights. Instead they were notable for their utterly vicious actions and behavior.[75] Second, in a related vein, it needs to be underscored that Pakistan actively undermined pro-independence organizations within Kashmir, such as the Jammu and Kashmir Liberation Front,

---

72  For a discussion see C. Christine Fair and Sumit Ganguly, "Lives on the Line," *The Washington Quarterly* 36, no. 3 (Summer 2013): 173–184.
73  S.M. Burke, *Mainsprings of Indian and Pakistani Foreign Policies* (Lahore: Oxford University Press, 1975).
74  For two recent accounts of the 1971 crisis see Bass, 2013. Also see Raghavan, 2013.
75  On this subject see the accounts in Adrian Levy and Cathy Scott-Clark, *The Meadow: Kashmir 1995 – Where the Terror Began* (London: HarperPress, 2012).

an avowedly secular party seeking self-determination. Instead its support went to those who had an explicitly pro-Pakistani agenda and did not even profess to speak for the Kashmiris.[76]

India, on the other hand, has never sought to pursue territorial aggrandizement. Even after it decisively defeated Pakistan in 1971 it did not seek to augment any territory in either battle sector. It withdrew its forces from the eastern sector, where it had helped create the new state of Bangladesh, with remarkable dispatch. Earlier, in the 1965 war, when it had seized the strategic Haji Pir Pass in Kashmir, despite the advice of the Indian military, Indian policy-makers chose to return it to Pakistan.[77]

The only instance of Indian territorial acquisition is the case of the Siachen Glacier dispute. In this case, when confronted with evidence of Pakistan-sponsored mountaineering expeditions, Indian policy-makers mounted a pre-emptive operation to establish a military outpost on the glacier in 1984. What had prompted India to mount an expensive and difficult military operation to seize the glacier? According to most accounts it can be traced to increasing information that Pakistan had been sponsoring expeditions to the glacier and that a number of international publications had been depicting the glacier as Pakistani territory.[78] The other background factor that may have also influenced Indian strategic calculations was the construction of the Karakorum Highway linking Pakistan's Northern Areas with China's Xinjiang Province. Even though this project had started shortly after the 1965 Indo-Pakistani conflict it was only completed in 1978. New Delhi had repeatedly protested the building of this road link as it passed through disputed territory but to little avail.[79]

In an attempt to prevent Pakistan from establishing a legal claim to the glacier, Indian policy-makers, on the advice of some Indian

76 For the ISI's support for pro-Pakistani entities see Arif Jamal, *Call For Transnational Jihad: Lashkar-e-Taiba, 1985–2014* (Portland: Avantgarde Books, 2014), pp. 71–84.

77 Brines, 1968.

78 P.L. Bhola, "Indo-Pakistan Control March Over Siachen Glacier," *Indian Journal of Asian Affairs* 1, no. 1 (Summer 1988): 28–48.

79 For further details see Robert Wirsing, "The Siachen Glacier Dispute: The Strategic Dimension," *Strategic Studies* 12 (Autumn 1988): 38–54.

military personnel, chose to launch an operation that enabled them to establish a presence on the glacier. This effort, "Operation Meghdoot," proved successful and India thereafter established a more permanent presence on the glacier.[80] Pakistan subsequently undertook action of its own – "Operation Abadeel" – to try and dislodge the Indian forces.[81]

Since then attempts to demilitarize the glacier have proven mostly fruitless despite multiple rounds of negotiations. The failure to bring about demilitarization stems from two sources. First, the Indian military which, after the expenditure of considerable amounts of blood and treasure, remains loath to cede the glacier. Indeed there is some evidence that it has actually blocked attempts to reach an accord.[82] Second, it also involves the Pakistani military's unwillingness to demarcate the actual ground position line (AGPL) for fear that any such agreement would necessarily privilege India which holds the physical high ground. It should, however, be stated that the basis of the dispute must be traced to divergent interpretations of the extension of the 1949 Karachi Agreement and the subsequent Shimla Agreement, which extended what came to be known as the Line of Control (LoC; replacing the CFL) to the glacier.[83]

It is also necessary to address some other questionable charges, which Pakistani policy-makers often invoke. In this context it is important to forthrightly reject the oft-repeated assertion that India, despite its stated abhorrence of the use of force, resorted to arms against the Portuguese in Goa in 1960. From a strictly factual standpoint this claim is correct. However, the facts are far from self-evident and deserve a brief discussion. Prime Minister Nehru had

---

80  For details see Harish Kapadia, *Siachen Glacier: The Battle of Roses* (New Delhi: Rupa, 2010).

81  For a Pakistani perspective on the Siachen issue see Omer Farooq Zain, "Siachen Glacier Conflict: Discordant in Pakistan-India Reconciliation," *Pakistan Horizon* 59, no. 2 (April 2006): 73–82; also see Aarish U. Khan, "Siachen Glacier: Getting Past the Deadlock," *Spotlight on Regional Affairs* 31, no. 5 (May 2012): 1–25.

82  Steven I. Wilkinson, *Army and Nation: The Military and Indian Democracy Since Independence* (Cambridge, MA: Harvard University Press, 2015), p. 225.

83  For an Indian view see Lieutenant-General V.R. Raghavan, *Siachen: Conflict Without End* (New Delhi: Viking, 2002); for a Pakistani perspective see Javed Hussain, "The Fight for Siachen," *The Express Tribune*, April 22, 2012.

negotiated in good faith with the Salazar regime in attempts to persuade the Portuguese to give up their colonial appendage in Western India. However, the Portuguese proved to be utterly intransigent. Faced with growing criticism from several of his African nationalist compatriots about his inability to dislodge the Portuguese from Goa through diplomatic persuasion, Nehru reluctantly ordered the Indian Army to oust them.[84] India's actions were quite consistent with the needs of a postcolonial state that had to end the enclaves of colonial power on its territory. The criticisms that were leveled against India were both anachronistic and polemical.

Two other matters also need to be addressed directly. The first involves India's decision to absorb the Himalayan state of Sikkim into its domain in 1975. Some, including a prominent Indian commentator, have indeed argued that this amounted to an annexation.[85] Yet the fact remains that the vast majority of the small Himalayan state's population had little or no use for the feudal reign of the traditional ruler, the Chogyal, and voted to join India. Subsequently, the state has not seen any popular unrest, has an elected parliament and enjoys representation in the Indian national legislature in New Delhi.

The other case, of course, involved India's use of force to induce the Nizam of Hyderabad to accede to India in the aftermath of independence and partition. The Nizam, who was widely unpopular amongst his predominantly Hindu subjects, had entertained hopes of joining Pakistan even though his realm did not abut any segment of Pakistan's territory. When the Nizam adopted an intransigent stance to integration with India and allowed paramilitary organizations within the state to repress his Hindu population, Prime Minister Nehru ordered the Indian Army to enter his realm and coerce him to accede to India.[86]

Pakistani interlocutors, however, continue to dwell on both the Goa and the Sikkim episodes (even though neither of them

84 Arthur G. Rubinoff, *India's Use of Force in Goa* (Bombay: Popular Prakashan, 1971).
85 Sunanda K. Datta-Ray, *Smash and Grab: Annexation of Sikkim* (Delhi: Westland, 1984).
86 Mohammed Hyder, *October Coup: A Memoir of the Struggle for Hyderabad* (New Delhi: Roli Books, 2012).

have any bearing on Pakistan or the Kashmir dispute) as well as the Hyderabad episode, as evidence of India's expansionist proclivities.

Four key propositions undergird the analysis that follows in this book. First, the two states have significantly divergent conceptions of regional security. Specifically, in the aftermath of the 1971 war, Indian and Pakistani decision-makers reached markedly different conclusions about regional security. In Pakistan there was little or no introspection about the choices that led up to the crisis and the subsequent collapse of the country.[87] Instead a widespread myth about Indian perfidy came to dominate all political discussions and analyses of the 1971 war. Accordingly, Pakistani decision-makers, and especially the military establishment, argued that given India's willingness to dismember the Pakistani state the country now faced an existential threat from India. Consequently, hostility toward India became unremitting, thereby sustaining and deepening the existing sources of discord.

In India, on the other hand, the victory simply demonstrated the hollowness of the ideological basis of the Pakistani state. Religion alone had failed to serve as a force to provide for the unity of Pakistan. This issue was of vital importance because, for all practical purposes, it undermined Pakistan's irredentist claim to Kashmir.[88] Simultaneously, even from a material standpoint, Pakistan ceased to be as great a threat as before because of its diminished capabilities.[89]

Second, in a related vein these beliefs came to be shared quite widely across the political spectrum in both states. For Pakistani policy-makers the defeat in 1971 was a matter to be avenged at any available chance. Consequently, when internal tensions arose

---

87 For the most thoughtful discussion of the break-up of Pakistan see Hasan Zaheer, *The Rise and Realization of Bengali Muslim Nationalism* (New York: Oxford University Press, 1997).

88 For a trenchant statement of this subject see Pran Nath Chopra, *India's Second Liberation* (Cambridge, MA: MIT Press, 1974).

89 This perception, however, would prove to be short-lived given Pakistan's subsequent acquisition of a nuclear arsenal, its forging of a strategic partnership with the PRC and its adoption of an asymmetric war strategy.

in the Indian Punjab in the early 1980s and in Kashmir in the late 1980s, they lost no opportunity to foment further discord.[90] Pakistani meddling in these two indigenous insurgencies, in turn led Indian decision-makers to see the adversary as implacable especially since Pakistan had no moral, let alone legal, basis to interfere in the domestic politics of Punjab.

Third, as a consequence of the first two factors, Pakistani decision-makers sought to forge a military doctrine that would enable them to cope with India's more substantial conventional capabilities.[91] To that end, given India's fraught relationship with the PRC, they made their country a vital strategic asset for the PRC in South Asia, simultaneously embarked on a clandestine nuclear weapons program and revived their use of asymmetric capabilities.[92] The growth of the Sino-Pakistani strategic nexus and Pakistan's active pursuit of a clandestine nuclear weapons program, in turn precipitated a nuclear rivalry with India. The use of asymmetric capabilities in conjunction with their nuclear arsenal created a dilemma for India because a conventional Indian military retaliation could result in nuclear escalation.[93]

Fourth, Pakistani decision-makers have learnt how to deftly manipulate this fear. To that end they have precipitated more than one crisis in the hope that great powers, most notably the United States, will step in to ward off the possibility of escalation. This strategy has been designed to keep the pressure on India on the unresolved Kashmir question. More recently, thanks to a host of terrorist organizations that Pakistan has helped spawn, nurture and support, it has been able to pursue a wider asymmetric war strategy against India. The Lashkar-e-Taiba (LeT) led attack on Bombay (Mumbai) in November 2008 was emblematic of this new strategy designed to bleed India with a "war of a thousand cuts."

90 On Pakistani involvement in the Kashmir insurgency see Ganguly, 1997.
91 For a careful analysis of the limits of India's conventional advantages see Walter C. Ladwig III, "Indian Military Modernization and Conventional Deterrence in South Asia," *Journal of Strategic Studies* (May 2015): 1–4.
92 On Pakistan's use of asymmetric warfare see Swami, 2007.
93 For a forceful statement of this argument see S. Paul Kapur, *Dangerous Deterrent: Nuclear Weapons Proliferation and Conflict in South Asia* (Stanford: Stanford University Press, 2007). Kapur, however, quite mistakenly argues that Pakistan adopted this strategy as it acquired a nuclear arsenal.

## A TROUBLED DECADE

Since the Kargil conflict of 1999, despite periodic tensions and the onset of at least two crises in 2001–2 and 2008, war did not erupt between the two adversaries. However, the efforts at peacemaking and conflict resolution, which have included unilateral Indian concessions, have also not been especially fruitful. Consequently, this decade can be carefully examined to test the propositions discussed earlier.

During this time span Pakistan had a democratic government twice, witnessed a military coup in October 1999 and also saw the end of the military regime in August 2008. In India, the period saw the alternation of democratic governments from the Bharatiya Janata Party (BJP) led National Democratic Alliance (NDA), to the Congress-led United Progressive Alliance (UPA). Ironically, according to multiple sources, both Indian and Pakistani, the two sides came close to reaching a rapprochement during the long period of military rule in Pakistan. However, the ouster of General Musharraf left New Delhi with no viable negotiating partner. Discussions with the civilian regime of President Asif Ali Zardari had continued even after his ouster. However, the horrific terrorist attack on Bombay (Mumbai) in November 2008 effectively brought the talks to a close.

Though Prime Minister Manmohan Singh held back a military response to the terrorist attack, the prospects of a meaningful dialogue were seriously undermined. Public opinion in India became dramatically inflamed in the wake of the attacks and significantly limited the prime minister's room for political maneuver. Consequently, while there were multiple attempts at renewing the discussions, for example on the sidelines of multilateral forums, these attempts did not make much headway.[94] Indeed it was not until February 2010 that the two sides agreed to renew the dialogue.[95]

A closer examination of the historical record suggests that Pakistan had long pursued this asymmetric war strategy. It simply revived and escalated it as circumstances proved more propitious; also see Vipin Narang, "Posturing for Peace? Pakistan's Nuclear Postures and South Asian Security," *International Security* 34, no. 3 (Winter 2009/10): 38–78.

94 Neil MacFarquhar, "India and Pakistan Fail to Restart Negotiations,"
   *New York Times*, September 27, 2009.
95 Lydia Polgreen, "India Offers to Renew Talks with Pakistan," *New York Times*,
   February 4, 2010.

## ENSUING CONSEQUENCES

If the relationship was indeed a *security dilemma* then presumably it could be ameliorated. They could, at the outset, foreswear any statements that might suggest a desire for territorial aggrandizement. One or both states could undertake measures that sought to reassure the other that its capabilities are strictly for defensive ends. They could also avoid such deployments that could be construed as being especially threatening or destabilizing.[96]

Indeed, the evidence does suggest that on a number of occasions India has sought to reassure Pakistan. As mentioned earlier in this chapter it returned the strategic Haji Pir Pass to Pakistan after the 1965 war. Earlier it had referred the Kutch dispute to the International Court of Justice and accepted the court's verdict even though the final judgment had proven favorable to Pakistan. Even after the outbreak of the Kashmir insurgency, after it had managed to establish a modicum of order in the portion of the state under its control, it chose to withdraw at least two divisions of Indian troops from forward deployments.[97]

None of these efforts, however, has elicited any meaningful cooperative responses from Pakistan. The military-dominated state, instead, has remained fixated on its central goal, namely, to pry Kashmir from the Indian Union, whether through conventional or asymmetric warfare.[98] Nor, for that matter, has its overall hostility toward India diminished.

## ORGANIZATION

The rest of this book will demonstrate that the Pakistani military's fixation with India mostly explains the persistence of this adversarial relationship. In the absence of a significant internal transformation of extant political arrangements of the Pakistani polity, it appears unlikely that any accommodation can be reached between these two long-standing rivals.

96 For a theoretical discussion see Jervis, 1976, pp. 167–214.
97 Amy Waldman, "India to Reduce Its Troop Strength in Kashmir," *New York Times*, November 12, 2004.
98 Fair, 2014.

Alternatively, the capabilities of the two states may diverge so dramatically that despite Pakistan's unwillingness to abandon its commitment to wrest the Indian-controlled portion of Kashmir through force, its efforts to this end will become increasingly meaningless. Under those circumstances the rivalry, for all practical purposes, would cease to matter.

The book is divided into six other chapters. Chapter 2 focuses on sources and outcomes of the Kargil War of 1999. Chapter 3 provides an account of the key developments in the Indian-controlled portion of the state of Kashmir during the decade under examination. Chapter 4 examines the attack on the Indian parliament in December 2001 and the onset of the 2001–2 crisis. Chapter 5 traces the origins of the "composite dialogue" and its eventual collapse. In Chapter 6 there is an examination of how the locus of the rivalry has now extended into Afghanistan. The final chapter, Chapter 7, discusses the policy implications that flow from the analysis of the developments of the decade.

# 2

# Kargil and after

In the early hours of May 5, 1999, an Indian Army patrol from the 121st Brigade was sent out on a routine reconnaissance mission in the Kaksar region along the LoC in Kashmir. This area, in turn, is located within the region of Kargil, a particularly forbidding and unforgiving stretch of territory located within the district of Ladakh in the Indian-controlled portion of the state of Jammu and Kashmir. The mountainous peaks in this region range from 16,000 to 18,000 feet.

When the patrol failed to return, the commanders of the brigade enhanced their reconnaissance of the area. To their shock and dismay they discovered that there were about 100 intruders along various mountain peaks near Kargil. Initially they concluded that they possessed sufficient capabilities to dislodge the infiltrators. However, by mid-May they had dramatically altered their initial estimate when they concluded that as many as 800 intruders were in the area. Worse still, toward the end of the month they concluded that as many as 70 positions across the LoC had been breached.[1]

Over the next several months India's armed forces had to mount a substantial air and ground counteroffensive to dislodge the invaders. In fact, this was the first occasion on which the IAF carried out

---

1 Sumit Ganguly, *Conflict Unending: India-Pakistan Tensions Since 1947* (New York: Columbia University Press, 2001).

military operations against Pakistani forces since the Indo-Pakistani war in 1971. The fighting did not conclude until the end of July despite a gradual withdrawal of hostile forces from about mid-July. The end of these military operations effectively concluded the fourth Indo-Pakistan conflict and the third one over the disputed state of Jammu and Kashmir.[2]

The Kargil incursions had come in the aftermath of what Indian policy-makers had believed was a highly successful summit in Lahore, the capital of the Pakistani Punjab in February 1999. Prime Minister Atal Behari Vajpayee of India has chosen to initiate a dialogue with Pakistan in the wake of the global outcry following the Indian and Pakistani nuclear tests of 1998. The occasion chosen for his visit was the launch of a new bus service linking Lahore with the Indian city of Amritsar.

In Lahore he had worked out a series of nuclear confidence building measures (CBMs) with his counterpart, Prime Minister Nawaz Sharif of Pakistan, based upon months of prior preparation. These nuclear CBMs were significant. Specifically, they had created a joint working group of technical experts and officials to negotiate an agreement on mutual strategic restraints. Additionally, they had agreed that neither country would intrude into each other's airspace, that they would hold military exercises at stipulated distances from the international border, to establish hotlines between the headquarters of their respective armed forces, the offices of their foreign secretaries and their prime ministers.[3]

He had also publicly reiterated India's commitment to Pakistan's integrity at the Minar-e-Pakistan, the site of the Lahore Resolution of 1940, which is widely considered to be the clarion call for the founding of the Pakistani state. In his speech, Vajpayee had categorically stated that, "A stable, secure and prosperous Pakistan is in our interest."[4]

The site of his speech was obviously fraught with much symbolic significance. More to the point, however, the fact that these words

---

2 For a discussion of all four wars see Ganguly, 2001.
3 J.N. Dixit, *India-Pakistan in War and Peace* (New Delhi: Books Today, 2002), p. 349.
4 For the full text see: *Associated Press of Pakistan News Summary*, February 22, 1999, http://fas.org/news/pakistan/1999/990222-appday.htm.

came from the prime minister who was a member of India's most jingoistic political party, the BJP, gave them added weight. In effect, Vajpayee had made it resolutely clear that his government was endorsing Pakistan's existence, thereby addressing a long-standing concern. Vajpayee's actions and words were nothing short of bold and could have constituted a watershed in Indo-Pakistani relations. Unfortunately, thanks to the Kargil incursions, his attempt to foster a new climate of trust and thereby open up the prospect of serious negotiations came to an abrupt close. Having staked a great deal of domestic political capital in undertaking this dramatic trip to Pakistan, it is wholly understandable that he saw the Kargil episode as a fundamental breach of trust.[5]

The breakdown of trust was all the more significant in that after the Lahore meeting, Sharif and Vajpayee had set up a back channel for discussions and had appointed trusted interlocutors to seek a possible solution to the Kashmir conundrum. Sharif had designated Niaz Naik, a distinguished former Pakistani diplomat, and Vajpayee appointed R.K. Mishra, a journalist of long repute. The decision to bypass formal channels of diplomatic intercourse was far from trivial. Both leaders had feared that their respective bureaucracies would lack the willingness to depart from long-held and mostly rigid positions.

Naik and Mishra apparently met from April 27 to May 1 in New Delhi. Through intense discussions and a rejection of a host of possible solutions they had come to the beginnings of a shared set of negotiating points, the crux of which lay in the delineation of a firm new international border. The question, of course, was where that border would be drawn. In the event, thanks to the discovery of the Kargil intrusions, the progress that had been made in this important back channel discussion was wholly lost.[6]

---

5 Nicholas J. Wheeler, "'I Had Gone to Lahore With a Message of Goodwill But in Return We Got Kargil': The Promise and Perils of 'Leaps of Trust' in India-Pakistan Relations," *India Review* 9, no. 3 (July–September 2010): 319–344; the sense of betrayal and a breach of trust are also recorded in Jaswant Singh, *A Call to Honour: In Service of Emergent India* (New Delhi: Rupa and Company, 2006).

6 For a detailed discussion of these talks see Owen Bennett Jones, *Pakistan: Eye of the Storm* (New Haven: Yale University Press, 2002), pp. 94–96.

SEEKING EXPLANATIONS

Why did Vajpayee's attempt to usher in a new era in Indo-Pakistani relations fail so abjectly? It is entirely understandable that a single dramatic gesture alone could not dispense with nearly six decades of almost unremitting mutual hostility. That said, the response to this move should not have culminated in the launching of a covert operation against India. The Pakistani response certainly appears to undermine the expectations of the *spiral model*. At a bare minimum, Vajpayee's willingness to open himself to domestic criticism should have at least prompted his Pakistani counterparts to take his initiative seriously and explore if his overture could lead to the genesis of a rapprochement. Instead his costly signal was wholly spurned.

Why then did the Pakistani regime respond in the fashion that it did? The explanation must be sought in the structure of the country's domestic politics. The civilian regime may notionally exercise control over the country's foreign relations. However, on all crucial decisions, the military establishment, which remains *primus inter pares*, can either undermine or simply overrule its choices. In few areas is this tendency to intervene in the country's fundamental foreign policy choices more pronounced than in the realm of Indo-Pakistan relations.[7]

The available evidence suggests that Prime Minister Nawaz Sharif may have been briefed about a possible military operation in Kargil. However, it is far from clear that he had inquired about or fully grasped the dimensions thereof. According to one Pakistani scholar he was given a full briefing on May 16, 1999. However, far from criticizing the infiltration apparently Sharif chose to seize upon the army chief's agenda and make it his own in an effort to refocus international attention on the Kashmir issue.[8] This action may well reek of rank political opportunism. However, it should be made clear that even if he had been fully apprised of the military's plans in advance there was not much that he could have done

---

7 For a thoughtful discussion see Hasan-Askari Rizvi, "Civil-Military Relations in Contemporary Pakistan," *Survival* 40, no. 2 (1998): 96–113.

8 Ayesha Jalal, *The Struggle for Pakistan: A Muslim Homeland and Global Politics* (Cambridge, MA: Harvard University Press, 2014).

to bring a halt to their realization. As argued earlier, the security establishment within Pakistan, because of its entrenched privileges within the political order, can effectively ignore the views of even a legitimately elected civilian regime.[9] As one observer of South Asian regional security issues has written:

The army and its intelligence arms, particularly the Inter-Services Intelligence Directorate (ISI), have never ceased to vie with the civilian bureaucracies for control over government policy in the crucial domain of national security, including Kashmir ... The requirement for absolute secrecy, paramount in an operation of this kind, would inevitably have constricted further a process of consultation already severely attenuated in Pakistan's politically hazardous institutional environment.[10]

In the event, the Pakistani military establishment had planned an operation that was designed to seize significant areas near the LoC to gain militarily advantageous positions overlooking India's National Highway, NH-1A, an arterial road connecting the state capital Srinagar to Leh, a regional hub.[11] The motivations for this operation and its timing remain the subject of debate especially given the paucity of reliable Pakistani sources. However, the available evidence suggests that the plan had been in the offing since India's successful launch of "Operation Meghdoot" and the seizure of the Siachen Glacier in 1984.[12] According to a highly reliable source, the initial operational plans for this endeavor had been drawn up as early as 1996.[13] The precise timing of the operation, however, could be attributed to tensions in civil–military relations within Pakistan under Prime Minister Nawaz Sharif and General Pervez Musharraf's desire to assert the military's prerogatives. It was also a function of the military's desire to impose costs on India

9  For a discussion of the extent and scope of Sharif's likely knowledge about the operation see Amarinder Singh, *A Ridge Too Far: War in the Kargil Heights 1999* (Patiala: Moti Bagh Palace, 2001), p. 35.

10  Robert G. Wirsing, *Kashmir in the Shadow of War: Regional Rivalries in a Nuclear Age* (Armonk: M.E. Sharpe, 2003), p. 47.

11  John H. Gill, "Military Operations in the Kargil Conflict," in Peter Lavoy (ed.), *Asymmetric Warfare in South Asia* (New York: Cambridge University Press, 2009).

12  V.R. Raghavan, *Siachen: Conflict Without End* (New Delhi: Viking Books, 2002).

13  Jones, 2002, pp. 92–93.

at a vulnerable time, that made the move salient as a counter to
the latter's military advantages in the Neelum Valley.[14] Finally,
some accounts suggest that the Pakistani military, as in the past,
had gambled that the incursion would once again focus attention on the Kashmir dispute and that the international community
would become involved in settling the dispute on terms favorable
to Pakistan.[15]

The incursions were bold but based upon a series of flawed
assumptions.[16] First, the military had believed that Indian forces,
which were tied down in counterinsurgency operations in Kashmir,
would be unable to mount a vigorous response to the incursions.
Second, they had assumed that India would be loath to engage in
either horizontal or vertical escalation for fear that the spiral could
culminate in the use of nuclear weapons. Third, they had underesti-
mated India's ability to bolster its capabilities along the LoC at short
notice given the extraordinarily harsh and unforgiving terrain that
they had to traverse. Fourth, as on a number of past occasions, the
Pakistani military leadership had counted on the international community and, most importantly, the United States to step in and bring
about a swift end to any conflict that might ensue. Fifth and finally,
there is little question that Pakistan's possession of nuclear weapons
had emboldened its military leadership. Given their innate proclivity toward seeking any possible avenue to revive the Kashmir question and also challenge India militarily, the acquisition of nuclear
weapons had provided them with a perceived advantage over India's
conventional capabilities. If India chose to embark on a strategy of
substantial conventional retaliation they were now in a position to
invoke the threat of the use of nuclear weapons.[17]

14  Feroz Hasan Khan, Peter R. Lavoy and Christopher Clary, "Pakistan's
    Motivations and Calculations," in Lavoy, 2009.
15  Howard B. Schaffer and Teresita C. Schaffer, *How Pakistan Negotiates with the
    United States: Riding the Roller Coaster* (Washington, DC: The United States
    Institute of Peace, 2011).
16  These misperceptions are rooted in what is referred to in the literature on
    political psychology as "motivated biases." For a discussion see Robert Jervis,
    Richard Ned Lebow and Janice Gross Stein, *Psychology and Deterrence*
    (Baltimore: Johns Hopkins University Press, 1985).
17  For a state and elaboration of this argument see S. Paul Kapur, *Dangerous
    Deterrent: Nuclear Weapons Proliferation and Conflict in South Asia*
    (Stanford: Stanford University Press, 2007).

## THE ONSET OF WAR

How did the war unfold? The principal Pakistani force that was involved in the incursions was composed of units from the Northern Light Infantry (NLI). According to one source, they were drawn from 4, 5, 6 and 12 NLI battalions. They initially occupied as many as 130 posts in Indian-controlled Kashmir along a 150-kilometer salient penetrating as far as 8 kilometers across the LoC.[18] They were able to do so because the abandonment of these posts were part of standard operating procedure during the winter months. The Pakistanis had deftly occupied the Indian forward posts that were vacant without Indian knowledge or resistance.

Once the Indian political leadership ascertained the scope and the dimensions of the intrusions they moved with alacrity to respond to them. Given the high altitude where the intruders had lodged themselves, policy-makers realized that the Indian Army would not be able to swiftly launch direct assaults on the occupied areas as troops from the plains would need time to be physically acclimatized.[19] Despite this knowledge, mostly gleaned from the disastrous experience of the Indian Army during the 1962 Sino-Indian border war, apparently some units were moved in haste and with predictably adverse consequences for the troops.[20]

Accordingly, for the first time since the 1971 war, India chose to use airpower against the well-entrenched Pakistani forces under the aegis of a military operation entitled "Operation Vijay" ("Operation Victory"). It is important to underscore that the IAF's eventual success came at some initial cost stemming from political, organizational and concomitant operational considerations. Initially, both the Indian Minister for External Affairs, Jaswant Singh, and the Chief of Air Staff, Air Marshal A.Y. Tipnis, were opposed to the

---

18  Marcus P. Acosta, "The Kargil Conflict: Waging War in the Himalayas," *Small Wars and Insurgencies* 18, no. 3 (September 2007): 397–415.

19  India's policy-makers had only partially learnt the appropriate lessons from the disastrous experience of the 1962 war when Indian troops were airlifted to high altitudes at short notice and with disastrous medical consequences. See Major-General D.K. Palit, *War in the High Himalaya: The Indian Army in Crisis* (London: C. Hurst and Company, 1991).

20  Acosta, 2007, p. 406.

use of airpower because they feared that it would be construed in Pakistan as a dramatically escalatory step.[21] Air Headquarters received an initial request for armed helicopter support in the Batalik Sector as early as May 1. At this time the army was advised to use artillery and then seek air power. On May 11, the army again requested the use of attack helicopters. This time Air Headquarters asked for a more detailed appreciation of the prevailing conditions. Also, it argued that attack helicopters would be vulnerable to surface air defenses. This may have been prompted with the attack on a helicopter on May 12 even though it managed to land safely with a damaged rotor.[22]

Furthermore, the Air Force was unwilling to go ahead and allow heliborne attacks without the express sanction of the government. To compound matters, the Chief of Army Staff, General V.P. Malik, was out of the country until May 20. He returned on May 21 and then visited the forward areas on May 23. Almost immediately, he concluded that without the use of airpower the intruders could not be dislodged. Accordingly, on May 24 he discussed the prevailing situation with the Chief of Air Staff, Air Marshal Tipnis. On May 25 they presented their arguments and evidence to the Cabinet Committee on Security (CCS). Based on their views the CCS authorized the use of the IAF but with the clear stipulation that the LoC was not to be crossed.[23]

On May 26, the IAF carried out its initial sorties. A day later it launched a second round of attacks with the aim of dislodging the Pakistani intruders from Batalik, Turtuk and Dras.[24]

---

21 Kartik Bommakanti, "Coercion and Control: Explaining India's Victory at Kargil," *India Review* 10, no. 3 (July–September 2011): 297.

22 Benjamin S. Lambeth, *Airpower at 18,000 Feet: The Indian Air Force in the Kargil War* (Washington, DC: Carnegie Endowment for International Peace, 2012), p. 10.

23 R. Sukumaran, "The 1962 India-China War and Kargil 1999: Restrictions on the Use of Air Power," *Strategic Analysis* 27, no. 3 (July–September 2003): 332–355; also see the discussion in General V.P. Malik, *Kargil: From Surprise to Victory* (New Delhi: HarperCollins, 2006).

24 The literature on the Kargil War is substantial. Unfortunately, it is almost exclusively one-sided and from the victorious Indian side. See for example, Kanti Bajpai, Afsir Karim and Amitabh Mattoo (eds.), *Kargil and After: Challenges for Indian Policy* (New Delhi: Har-Anand, 2001); Lieutenant-General Y.M. Bammi, *Kargil: The Impregnable Conquered* (Noida: Gorkha Publishers, 2002); Srinjoy Chowdhury, *Despatches from*

It is important to underscore that IAF pilots were under strict instructions not to cross the LoC in Kashmir.[25] It is widely believed that these instructions were issued to avoid possible vertical escalation of the conflict. Apart from this politically imposed hindrance, the IAF faced other important constraints on its actions. The NLI possessed surface-to-air missiles (SAM), the IAF's primary attack helicopter, a Russian-origin, Mi-35 HIND was too heavy to fly at high altitudes, the thin air reduced the accuracy of aerial weaponry and the terrain facilitated the concealment of Pakistani SAM batteries.[26]

Two highly informed analysts have written about the air campaign referred to as "Operation Safed Sagar" ("white ocean") as follows:

During the air campaign, the IAF gained the ability to improvise new bombing techniques and methods of attack. The willingness and ability to innovate paid handsome dividends. The sustained air strikes came as a surprise to Pakistani planners who had not vectored such determined Indian response into their calculations. The air strikes had an extremely detrimental psychological impact on the enemy troops who found themselves powerless to retaliate against death and destruction being rained down on them from a distance.[27]

*Kargil* (New Delhi: Penguin Books, 2000); Major-General Ashok Krishna and P.R. Chari (eds.), *Kargil: The Tables Turned* (New Delhi: Manohar, 2001); Malik, 2006; Singh, 2001; Jasjit Singh (ed.), *Kargil 1999: Pakistan's Fourth War for Kashmir* (New Delhi: Knowledge World, 1999); Praveen Swami, *The Kargil War* (New Delhi: LeftWord Books, 2000); Major-General Ashok Kalyan Verma, *Blood on the Snow: Tactical Victory and Strategic Failure* (New Delhi: Manohar Books, 2002); for an important Pakistani contribution see Brigadier-General Shaukat Qadir, "An Analysis of the Kargil Conflict 1999," *Journal of the Royal United Services Institution* 147, no. 2 (April 2002): 24–30.

25  Personal interview with IAF pilots, Washington, DC, November 2000. The decision was made at the highest political levels. Quite apart from the escalatory potential of such an action, it was also feared that the decision might precipitate a meeting of the United Nations Security Council (UNSC) leading to a call for a swift ceasefire. Personal interview, with senior, retired national security official, December 12, 2011, New Delhi.

26  Acosta, 2007, p. 405.

27  Let. Gen. (retd.) V.K. Sood and Pravin Sawhney, *Operation Parakram: The War Unfinished* (New Delhi: Sage, 2003), p. 71.

The IAF's success came about as a consequence of the ingenuity of its pilots. They carefully aimed projectiles designed to initiate landslides and avalanches, they carried out nighttime combat operations and used stopwatches and global positioning system receivers to navigate and acquire targets at night. They also introduced the Mirage 2000 into combat. Since it was capable of delivering laser-guided munitions the accuracy of the air campaign increased dramatically.[28] With the use of airpower and subsequent ground assaults, the Indian forces made steady if dogged progress. In all, the IAF flew as many as 1,700 strikes, combat air patrols, escort and reconnaissance sorties throughout the campaign.[29] One critical and successful attack was on the principal administrative and logistical camp at Muntho Dhalo in the Batalik sector on June 17. This was the principal supply depot of the NLI and its destruction caused havoc on Pakistan's ability to sustain the war effort in Kargil.[30]

By the end of June, the Indian Army had managed to recapture some 21 positions. However, it was really not until around July 26 that the Indian Army had successfully driven all the Pakistani forces from isolated locations. According to one estimate, India lost 474 soldiers and suffered 1,109 wounded. Pakistan lost 700 soldiers and suffered over a thousand wounded.[31]

DIPLOMATIC OVERTURES

As Indian forces made progress on the ground, a more confident leadership invited the Pakistani Minister for Foreign Affairs, Sartaj Aziz, to New Delhi for talks. However, the Indian Minister for External Affairs, Jaswant Singh, made it amply clear prior to the talks that any possible discussions would be strictly confined to Pakistan's role in precipitating the Kargil crisis. In the event the talks were held on June 12 but quickly ended in an impasse as Indian and Pakistani negotiating positions were far apart. Aziz sought a "partial de-escalation" in Kargil and called for an end to Indian air strikes and artillery barrages. Furthermore, he claimed that the

---

28 Acosta, 2007, p. 407.    29 Lambeth, 2012, p. 22.
30 Lambeth, 2012, p. 20.    31 Acosta, 2007, p. 410.

regime in Islamabad had little or no control over the intruders. Singh, however, steadfastly refused to accept Aziz's proposal and, on the contrary, insisted that Pakistan withdraw its troops.[32]

In the meantime, Pakistan's "all-weather ally," the PRC, maintained a formal, neutral stance during the Kargil crisis.[33] Despite this overt diplomatic stance, in reality it was covertly supporting Pakistan. Some of the evidence is circumstantial and thereby inferential, while other elements that are more apparent reveal clear hostile intent. First, both General Musharraf and Prime Minister Nawaz Sharif visited Beijing after the commencement of hostilities in Kargil. Second, the People's Liberation Army's (PLA) director of the Department of Armament visited Islamabad during the war to assist Pakistan meet vital shortages of conventional weapons, ammunition and equipment. Third, the PLA significantly expanded its troop presence and patrolling along key positions along the disputed Sino-Indian border during much of the crisis.[34]

As Indian troops were making steady progress in dislodging the last Pakistani intruders, Nawaz Sharif sought a diplomatic pathway out of the crisis. To that end, he flew to Washington, DC and met with President Bill Clinton at Blair House on July 4. It is reasonable to surmise that Sharif, based upon the past experiences of various Pakistani leaders, had expected some commiseration if not outright support from the United States. More to the point, he had obviously discounted the significance of an earlier phone call that the president had placed on June 15 in which he had asked Sharif to withdraw his troops. Obviously, Sharif had placed much stock in US behavior in past crises, when attempts had been made to avoid placing the blame squarely on a single country. Such past experiences may well have led him to conclude that yet again the US would fail to adopt an unequivocal position on the dispute.

---

32 Jyoti Malhotra, "India Shoots Down Pak's 'Partial' Offer, Talks End," *The Indian Express*, June 13, 1999.

33 For the PRC's formal diplomatic stance, see Bhartendu Kumar Singh, "Chinese Views on the Kargil Conflict," *Institute of Peace and Conflict Studies*, New Delhi, June 25, 1999. Available at: www.ipcs.org/article_details .php?articleNo=211.

34 For details especially those pertaining to the PRC's increased aggressiveness along the border in the midst of the crisis see Malik, 2006, pp. 297–298.

If Sharif had expected any element of sympathy from Clinton he was quickly disabused of any such hope. Unlike in the past where the United States had either sided with Pakistan or had at least equivocated on the question of responsibility for the initiation of a war, President Clinton bluntly informed Sharif that he saw Pakistan as the initiator of the crisis. Worse still, Clinton informed Sharif that the "sanctity of the Line of Control" had to be upheld and that "borders cannot be re-drawn in blood."[35]

When the conflict drew to a close, the United States provided Nawaz Sharif a face-saving opportunity, namely its willingness to facilitate Indo-Pakistani negotiations over Kashmir. The BJP-led regime in the meanwhile, appointed a high level committee to examine the question of the dramatic intelligence failure that had led to the Kargil intrusions and to suggest measures, both military and institutional. To that end, on July 29, 1999 it asked a noted, former Indian bureaucrat who had spent the bulk of his career in the Ministry of Defense, K. Subrahmanyam, to chair the inquiry. The other members of the committee were retired Lieutenant-General K.K. Hazari, the noted journalist B.G. Verghese and Satish Chandra, a distinguished former Foreign Service Officer, who was designated as the Member-Secretary of the Committee.

### THE ROAD TO AGRA

Despite the setback of Kargil, Vajpayee made another attempt to improve relations with Pakistan. To that end he invited General Musharraf to Agra in May 2001 for a bilateral summit. What prompted him to invite Musharraf to Agra despite his deep sense of betrayal in the wake of the Kargil War? The most forthright account of his decision to renew a dialogue with General Musharraf can be gleaned from the diplomatic memoirs of a respected, former Indian Foreign Secretary and, subsequently, National Security Adviser, Jyotirindra Nath Dixit. Dixit argues that Vajpayee initially wanted to meet Musharraf on the sidelines of some multilateral forum.

---

35  For a discussion of the Clinton-Sharif meeting at Blair House see Bruce Reidel, *American Diplomacy and the 1999 Kargil Summit at Blair House* (Philadelphia: University of Pennsylvania Press, 2002). Reidel, a former CIA officer, was the note-taker at this meeting.

However, his Union Home Minister and BJP stalwart, Lal Krishna Advani, persuaded him to hold a bilateral meeting instead.[36]

Other domestic developments also moved Vajpayee to break the existing deadlock. In 2000, thanks to an initiative on the part of Prime Minister Vajpayee, a three-month ceasefire was reached with one of the principal Kashmiri insurgent groups, the Hizb-ul-Mujahideen (HuM). However, at least two other Pakistan-based and supported terrorist organizations, the LeT and the Jaish-e-Mohammed (JeM), categorically refused to accede to the ceasefire arrangements. Consequently, even though representatives of the Hizb started negotiations with New Delhi through chosen interlocutors, the talks made little headway.[37] Specifically, attempts at bringing about ceasefires within Kashmir had proved to be unfruitful, and infiltration from Pakistan had continued unabated.[38]

Furthermore, there is some evidence that the United States had also gently prodded both parties toward renewing a bilateral dialogue.[39] For his part, President Musharraf had apparently concluded that the United States, after long having been sympathetic toward Pakistan on the Kashmir question, was now shifting its position in a more pro-Indian direction.[40] Such an inference was hardly unreasonable. The United States had adopted an explicitly pro-Indian stance during the Kargil War and was none too pleased with General Musharraf's coup of October 1999.[41] Furthermore, the coup had led to another layer of sanctions in addition to the ones that were already in place. To add to Pakistan's sense of isolation, President Clinton had chosen to spend five days on his visit to India in 2000 and five hours in Islamabad.

---

36 Advani also insists in his autobiography that he was responsible for prodding Vajpayee to invite Musharraf to Agra. On this issue see L.K. Advani, *My Country, My Life* (New Delhi: Rupa & Co., 2010).

37 Dixit, 2002.   38 Dixit, 2002.

39 Rahul Bedi, "US has Strategic Interest in Agra Summit," *The Irish Times*, July 14, 2001.

40 Zafar Masud, "A General From Pakistan Could Do the Subcontinent a Favor," *The International Herald Tribune*, July 13, 2001.

41 Strobe Talbott, *Engaging India: Diplomacy, Democracy and the Bomb* (Washington, DC: The Brookings Institution, 2004).

At a domestic level, Musharraf also faced certain pressures to try and ease tensions with India. Specifically, the country's economy was in dire straits. Indeed, a few weeks prior to the summit Musharraf had actually conceded on national television that Pakistan's security commitments were incompatible with its economic capabilities.[42]

Simultaneously, he was aware that his Indian counterparts were also more prone to the prospect of renewing the dialogue for domestic reasons. The insurgency in Kashmir had not ended, a ceasefire held with one of the principal terrorist organizations (the HuM) had failed, a unilateral Indian ceasefire had ended and an attempt at negotiations that a former Indian Minister of Defense, K.C. Pant, had led on behalf of the government had also reached an impasse.[43]

Despite these propitious conditions for resuming the dialogue, discordant notes, however, were evident even before the summit started. No doubt with an eye toward addressing his domestic constituency, President Musharraf had declared that Kashmir remained the "core issue" between India and Pakistan.[44] Furthermore, the Pakistan High Commission in New Delhi, much to the chagrin of the hosts, invited the leadership of the separatist All Party Hurriyat Conference (APHC), a loose conglomeration of political parties opposed to Indian rule in Jammu and Kashmir. The decision to invite them piqued the government in New Delhi because it had staunchly maintained that the APHC's views were not representative of most Kashmiris.[45]

Once in New Delhi, just prior to the summit, when faced with a battery of questions from Indian journalists about his characterization of Kashmir as a "core issue," Musharraf softened his stance. The summit, held on July 15 and 16 in the historic city of Agra,

---

42  Zahid Hussain, *Frontline Pakistan: The Struggle With Militant Islam*
    (New York: Columbia University Press, 2007), p. 104.

43  Aijaz Ahmad, "So Near, Yet So Far," *Frontline*, 18:15, July 21–August 3, 2001.

44  Shortly before the Agra Summit Musharraf had removed the largely ceremonial
    president of Pakistan, Rafiq Tarar, and had formally assumed the presidency. On
    the matter of Kashmir as the "core issue" see B. Muralidhar Reddy, "Kashmir
    will be Core Issue, Musharraf Tells Clerics," *The Hindu*, June 30, 2001.

45  Nirmal Ghosh, "Pragmatism Essential to India-Pakistan Détente," *The Straits
    Times*, July 11, 2001.

home of the spectacular Mughal monument, the Taj Mahal, started out on a hopeful note. It was also held under the glare of a newly emergent, and increasingly intrusive, Indian electronic media.

It is believed that the summit had made some progress on its initial day with a meeting between Prime Minister Vajpayee and President Musharraf. However, at the conclusion of the first day, the Minister of Information and Broadcasting, Sushma Swaraj, gave a briefing to India's state-owned television network, Doordarshan. In this press conference, she listed a series of subjects that the two leaders had apparently discussed. Conspicuous in its absence was the question of the Kashmir dispute. Almost immediately after her remarks speculation became rife about the seeming failure to include this critical question in the talks.

In the meantime the drafting of a joint declaration was well under way. However, it is believed that Minister for Home Affairs, Lal Krishna Advani, had expressed serious reservations about the failure to include some reference to the issue of cross-border terrorism in the joint declaration. As a consequence, on the evening of July 16, for all practical purposes, the talks reached a deadlock.[46]

Much has been written about the reasons for the eventual collapse of the summit.[47] There is little question that, in part, it failed to make any meaningful progress largely because there were fundamental differences within the Indian elite. Specifically, Prime Minister Atal Behari Vajpayee and his Minister for External Affairs, Jaswant Singh were more prone to making substantive concessions to Pakistan, especially on the vexed question of the Kashmir dispute. However, the Minister for Home Affairs, Lal Krishna Advani, had adopted a more intransigent position on the subject. More to

---

46 For one view which suggests that Swaraj helped to deliberately torpedo the talks see Asma Jehangir, "Agra Summit Produced Some Dividends for India and Pakistan," *Independent*, July 31, 2001; also see the discussion in A.G. Noorani, "The Truth about Agra," *Frontline*, 22:15, July 16–29, 2005. Noorani contends that both Sushma Swaraj and Lal Kishen Advani were instrumental in scuttling the talks because of their basic intransigence toward President Musharraf and Pakistan.

47 For two competing views see, HT Correspondent, "Agra Summit Failed Due to Indian Official," *The Hindustan Times*, December 4, 2010 and TNN, "General's Stand on Terrorism Derailed Agra Summit," *The Economic Times*, September 27, 2006.

the point, he was insistent that the final communiqué include some reference to Pakistan's abetment of terror in Kashmir.[48] Following the breakdown of the talks there were some desultory statements about the possible resumption of the talks and also mutual recriminations for their breakdown.[49] However, little substantive progress took place. Instead there were mutual accusations of provocative troop movements in Jammu and Kashmir. Despite this fraught atmosphere, Vajpayee and Musharraf agreed to meet at the United Nations General Assembly session on September 25, 2001.

This meeting, however, was not to take place. In the aftermath of the terrorist attacks on the United States on September 11, 2001, the proposed meeting was cancelled. In the wake of the terrorist attacks, Pakistan, which had enjoyed excellent ties with the Taliban regime in Afghanistan, came under unrelenting American pressure to fundamentally alter its policies.[50] Faced with inexorable American pressure, President Musharraf made a public volte-face.[51] He agreed to end support for the Taliban regime and to cooperate with the United States to help eviscerate Al Qaeda. However, there is incontrovertible evidence that his regime did not terminate its ties to the Taliban long after its publicly stated willingness to do so.

India, for its part, not only expressed its sympathy for the victims of the terrorist attack but in a remarkable development also offered

48  Interview with senior retired Indian intelligence official, New Delhi, November 16, 2010.

49  John Cherian, "Pakistani Perceptions," *Frontline*, 18:16, August 4–17, 2001; for an authoritative Pakistani view of the breakdown of the summit see Abdul Sattar, *Case Study on Comparisons of Lahore, Agra and Islamabad Summits* (Lahore: Pakistan Institute of Legislative Development and Transparency, 2004); Sattar, a professional diplomat, served both as Pakistan's Foreign Secretary and subsequently as its Minister for Foreign Affairs.

50  The best treatment of Pakistan's ties to the Taliban remains Ahmed Rashid, *Taliban: Militant Islam, Oil and Fundamentalism in Central Asia* (New Haven: Yale University Press, 2001); also see Larry Goodson, *Afghanistan's Endless War: State Failure, Regional Politics and the Rise of the Taliban* (Seattle: University of Washington Press, 2001).

51  For details of the pressure that had been brought to bear on Musharraf see Bruce Reidel, *Deadly Embrace: Pakistan, America and the Future of the Global Jihad* (Washington, DC: The Brookings Institution, 2011), p. 65.

the United States access to its military bases for prosecuting military action against the Taliban regime in Afghanistan. The United States, however, did not accept the Indian offer and instead chose to rely on Pakistan to carry out military operations in Afghanistan.

Within a month, Indo-Pakistan relations, which were already strained, took a turn for the worse on October 1. A suicide bomb attack on the Jammu and Kashmir state assembly building took the lives of some 38 individuals. The Pakistan-based terrorist organization, JeM, claimed responsibility for this attack.[52]

### SEARCHING FOR OPTIONS

In the wake of the Kargil War, while efforts were made to renew discussions with Pakistan, Indian policy-makers and key members of the military also sought to forge a new military doctrine. The Kargil conflict had not only amounted to a major intelligence failure, but it also underscored that despite the mutual acquisition of nuclear weapons, the possibility of war between the two adversaries nevertheless remained. The task for India's policy-makers was now to devise a strategy that would still provide a riposte against Pakistani incursions without the danger of escalation to a full-scale war. Pared to the bone they sought to formulate a doctrine and develop the requisite capabilities to parry Pakistan's reliance on its nuclear shield to provoke India with impunity using asymmetric forces. Indian policy-makers and strategists argued that this doctrine would enable them to fight a conventional war under a nuclear shadow.

George Fernandes, the Indian Minister of Defense, was the first significant official who enunciated the concept at a major international conference.[53] General Ved Prakash Malik, the Chief of Staff of the Indian Army during the Kargil War, also echoed Fernandes' views and became one of the most outspoken proponents of this

---

52 Praveen Swami, "An Audacious Strike," *Frontline*, 18:21, October 13–26, 2001.
53 George Fernandes, "The Challenges of Limited War: Parameters and Options," January 5, 2000. Inaugural address at a National Conference on "The Challenges of Limited War: Parameters and Options," January 5–6, 2000, New Delhi. Downloaded on May 6, 2011. Available at: www.idsa-india.org/defmin5-2000.html.

doctrine. He argued that contrary to a host of claims, the conduct of the Kargil War had demonstrated that it was possible to keep a conflict confined in both time and space.[54]

In subsequent writings and speeches, Malik went on to elaborate his views about how escalation could be controlled even in the context of a war between nuclear-armed adversaries. The crux of his argument can be summarized as follows. Any conflict that ensued would need to have limited political and military objectives, would not inflict inordinate pain on the adversary, and would be limited in geographic scope and time and in the levels of force that would be brought to bear.[55]

Malik's views and those of Fernandes, however, did not go unchallenged. Key individuals in India's defense policy community raised questions about the ability of decision-makers to control escalation in a nuclear context. Specifically, they argued that Indian and Pakistani decision-makers might have significant discrepancies between acceptable politico-military goals. Furthermore, they may disagree on thresholds that each side deems tolerable.[56]

Others also argued that the ability to keep any conflict limited was also quite questionable. They underscored the willingness of the Pakistani military apparatus to deliberately threaten escalation and its propensity for risk taking. Furthermore, they argued that these factors could contribute to miscalculation and thereby lead to uncontrolled escalation. Consequently, Indian plans to keep the conflict limited could be deliberately thwarted. Resultantly, they concluded that the pursuit of a limited war option could either fail in actually containing Pakistan's risk-prone behavior or worse still

---

54  For his views see General V.P. Malik, "The Challenges of Limited War: Parameters and Options," January 5–6, 2000. Closing address at a National Seminar on "The Challenges of Limited War: Parameters and Options," January 6, 2000, New Delhi. Downloaded on May 6, 2011. Available at: www.idsa-india.org/chief6-2000.html.

55  Malik's views were most clearly articulated at a seminar held at the Institute of Peace and Conflict Studies in New Delhi on November 30, 2004. See V.P. Malik, "Limited War and Escalation Control –I," Institute of Peace and Conflict Studies, New Delhi, November 30, 2004. Downloaded on May 5, 2011. Available at: www.ipcs.org/article/nuclear/limited-war-and-escalation-control-i-1570.html.

56  V.R. Rahgavan, "Limited War and Nuclear Escalation in South Asia," *The Nonproliferation Review* 8, no. 3 (Fall/Winter 2001): 16.

result in a full-scale war fraught with the possibility of nuclear usage.[57]

These reservations notwithstanding, Indian military planners continued to think of possible means to tackle Pakistan's asymmetric war strategy. Actually forging such a doctrine and an accompanying strategy would prove to be far more elusive and difficult. India's inability to respond became apparent in the wake of a terrorist attack on December 13, 2001. Despite all the discussion that had ensued in the wake of the Kargil War, the country lacked a contingency plan that it could rapidly implement to respond to this Pakistan-based terrorist strike, not to mention a credible deterrent against such action. Instead, as Chapter 3 will discuss, Indian policy-makers resorted to a lumbering mass mobilization to pursue a ham-handed strategy of coercive diplomacy.

CONCLUSIONS

An examination of the antecedents of the Kargil War and the unraveling of the Agra Summit both suggest that a straightforward *security dilemma* explanation cannot adequately explain the outcomes. In the case of Kargil, it is hard to identify any immediate military choices on the Indian side that may have precipitated the fears of the Pakistani military. Of course, it should be acknowledged that even a peace process that a civilian government entered into with India could be construed as a threat to its domestic prerogatives.

From another standpoint, as some scholars have argued, their overt acquisition of nuclear weapons may have actually emboldened them to undertake the venture, secure in the knowledge that India was unlikely to mount a substantial conventional response for fear of the dangers of nuclear escalation.[58]

Despite Pakistan's decisive defeat at India's hands in the 1971 war, the generous postwar settlement at the Shimla Conference in 1972[59]

57 Arzan Tarapore, *Holocaust or Hollow Victory: Limited War in Nuclear South Asia* (New Delhi: Institute of Peace and Conflict Studies, 2006).

58 This argument is developed in S. Paul Kapur, "India and Pakistan's Unstable Peace: Why Nuclear South Asia is Not Like Cold War Europe," *International Security* 30, no. 2 (Fall 2005): 127–152.

59 For contrasting Indian and Pakistani views on the accord See P.R. Chari and Pervaiz Iqbal Cheema, *The Simla Agreement 1972: Its Wasted Promise*

and no subsequent Indian efforts to threaten or coerce Pakistan, the vexed question of Kashmir[60] had continued to animate the Pakistani military.[61] Since 1989, as argued in an earlier chapter, the Pakistani security apparatus had sought to exploit India's malfeasances in Kashmir that had contributed to the insurgency. By the late 1990s, thanks to the growing sophistication and effectiveness of India's counterinsurgency strategy, the situation in Kashmir had become far more manageable.[62] More to the point, the global community had started to lose interest in the issue. Faced with this situation the Pakistani military chose to embark on a military adventure to see if it could again focus international attention on the matter while simultaneously attempting to improve its ground position in the region.

Consequently, the analysis in this chapter leads to the conclusion that neither a potential Indian threat through either weapons acquisitions nor through statements of hostile intent contributed to Pakistan's insecurity. Instead the willingness of the Pakistani military to exploit existing political cleavages within India to pursue its

---

(New Delhi: Manohar Books, 2001); Pakistan, apparently, did not deem the Shimla Accord to be especially generous. The Army, in particular, felt that it had been signed under duress as India was holding 93,000 prisoners of war. I am grateful to a retired, senior US military officer with substantial experience with South Asian issues for this particular insight. Personal correspondence, October 2014.

60  Of course throughout the decade of the 1990s Pakistan had been actively involved in providing support and sanctuaries to a host of anti-Indian terrorist organizations in Kashmir following the outbreak of an ethnoreligious insurgency in the state in 1989. On the origins of the Kashmir insurgency see Sumit Ganguly, *The Crisis in Kashmir: Portents of War, Hopes of Peace* (New York: Cambridge University Press, 1997); on Pakistan's involvement in Kashmir see Praveen Swami, *India, Pakistan and the Secret Jihad: The Covert War in Kashmir, 1947–2004* (London: Routledge, 2007).

61  The one possible exception might be India's initiation of Exercise Brasstacks in 1987. However, the exercise was conducted within a specific political and strategic context. The military regime of General Zia-ul-Haq had been aiding and abetting the indigenous insurgency in Punjab. One of the goals of this military exercise was to demonstrate that India could engage in strategic coercion even as it was battling the Sikh insurgents. For a detailed discussion of the Brasstacks crisis see Kanti Bajpai, P.R. Chari, Pervez Iqbal Cheema, Stephen P. Cohen and Sumit Ganguly, *Brasstacks and Beyond: Perception and the Management of Crisis in South Asia* (New Delhi: Manohar Books, 1995).

62  For details see Swami, 2007.

agenda in Kashmir contributed to tensions and culminated in the Kargil War.

Separately, it is evident that the structure of civil–military relations vitiated any notion that the politically legitimate authority within Pakistan was capable of making any decisions pertaining to critical questions of war and peace and thereby to mitigate possible escalatory effects. Nor, for that matter, were they capable of reining in the jihadi forces that had been so carefully nurtured over many years and then significantly boosted during the Afghan war years. With the return of military rule in Pakistan, the nexus between these jihadi organizations and the military was now strengthened.[63]

The Agra Summit's infelicitous conclusion also underscores the significance of critical policy differences within Indian policy-making elites. Despite Home Minister Advani's claim that he had no differences of opinion with Prime Minister Vajpayee, there is evidence that their positions on the question of Pakistan's abetment of terror were hardly identical. In fact, it is more than apparent that the two of them had fundamental differences on questions pertaining to the significance of the Kashmir dispute and the issue of Pakistan's involvement with terror. Not surprisingly, these led to an internal deadlock on the Indian side and thereby helped to undermine progress at the summit.[64]

There is no gainsaying that policy differences within the Indian elite contributed to a failure to engage Pakistan at the Agra summit. However, in closing this discussion it needs to be underscored that once again it was India that initiated the discussions with Pakistan. This dialogue had been set in motion despite the Pakistani security establishment's undermining of the Lahore peace process. Indeed

63  Vali Reza Nasr, "Military Rule, Islamism and Democracy in Pakistan," *Middle East Journal* 58, no. 2 (Spring 2004): 195–209.

64  On this subject see A.G. Noorani, "The Truth About Agra," *Frontline*, July 16–29, 2005. One does not have to fully accept Noorani's analysis and conclusion that Advani was intent on torpedoing the summit to argue that there were important policy differences within the BJP leadership. An interview with a former senior intelligence official confirmed that Advani had indeed stood his ground on the question of Pakistan's support for terror and had refused to allow the Kashmir question to become the primary focus of any joint communiqué. Personal interview with former senior intelligence official, New Delhi, October 21, 2010.

the Kargil War had highlighted the security establishment's intransigence toward any form of accommodation with India, let alone a proper rapprochement. The decision to launch a covert war against India again demonstrated that it was not reconciled to the status quo. If the Pakistani state, and in particular, the security establishment, was genuinely security seeking and not interested in territorial aggrandizement they would not have so carefully forged a plan to launch the war in the first place.

# 3

## The troubled decade in Kashmir

Despite the failure to refocus international attention on the Kashmir issue through the incursions in Kargil and its vicinity, Pakistan's decision-makers remained unwilling to abandon their claims or dispense with the asymmetric war strategy that they had long relied upon to provoke India. The Pakistani security establishment composed of the uniformed military and the intelligence services, despite this latest setback, did not in any way abandon its commitment to keep the Kashmir question alive. On the contrary it simply renewed its efforts to sustain the military pressures on India through the use of a range of proxy forces. When faced with significant external pressures coupled with domestic turmoil the military establishment, especially under General Musharraf, engaged India in a dialogue. However, as this and the subsequent chapter will demonstrate, it is far from clear that Musharraf enjoyed the support of the country's sprawling security establishment.[1] Consequently, even though the two parties arrived at a blueprint for embarking upon a process of rapprochement there is little or no evidence that Musharraf had succeeded in obtaining the assent of the military establishment. Without a clear-cut consensus within the military about a willingness to seek a rapprochement with India it is hard to imagine how

1 The only contrary claim can be found in Bruce Reidel, *Deadly Embrace: Pakistan, America and the Future of the Global Jihad* (Washington, DC: Brookings, 2011), p. 71. Even this claim is cryptic at best.

the Pakistani state could have made a binding, credible commitment on such a fraught and vexed issue.

Of course, it is important to underscore that such a shift in views would be quite contrary to the organizational ethos and beliefs of the military establishment. Having been long committed to a policy of unrelenting hostility toward India, in the absence of some dramatic endogenous or exogenous shock to their status and interests it could not reasonably be expected to abandon long-held commitments. Of course, shocks alone were unlikely to lead to a new fundamental recalculation of the military's interests and proclivities. The shocks would also have to be accompanied with the prospect of an alternative set of governing arrangements. Such a moment did seem to arise in the aftermath of the 1971 East Pakistan crisis. However, Zulfikar Ali Bhutto, the president of Pakistan, squandered that opportunity to consolidate democratic institutions.[2]

In the immediate aftermath of the Kargil War, with marked exceptions, the Pakistani security establishment remained quite prone to engage in various forms of myth-making to bolster its core strategic beliefs, especially to keep the Kashmir dispute alive at all costs. This can be clearly discerned from a number of sources and especially the self-exculpatory memoir of General Pervez Musharraf. Instead of accepting responsibility for a flawed and ultimately failed military operation, he sought to blame India for expanding the scope of the conflict.[3] Worse still, it became a virtual staple of most Pakistani analysts to argue that the Kargil episode was a tactical success but a strategic failure.[4] They thereby failed to recognize the fundamentally questionable value of the entire enterprise despite international disapprobation for having precipitated the crisis, their inability to seize any territory from India and the substantial loss of men and material. Furthermore, Prime Minister Nawaz Sharif's ouster in a

---

2  For a discussion of how shocks can create new expectations and thereby open up the possibility of significant political change see Karen Rasler, William R. Thompson and Sumit Ganguly, *How Rivalries End* (Philadelphia: University of Pennsylvania Press, 2013)

3  Pervez Musharraf, *In the Line of Fire: A Memoir* (New York: Free Press, 2006).

4  Ashley J. Tellis, C. Christine Fair and Jamison Jo Medby, *Limited Conflicts Under the Nuclear Umbrella: Indian and Pakistani Lessons from the Kashmir Crisis* (Santa Monica: RAND Corporation, 2001).

military coup from office in October 1999, effectively ensured that there would be little or no honest public discussion of the factors that had led up to the Kargil conflict and its aftermath.[5]

Their Indian counterparts, as discussed in the previous chapter, sought to devise a new military doctrine that would enable to them to fight a limited conventional war under the nuclear shadow. As they focused their energies on this effort they failed to embark on any endeavor that would enable them to drain the reservoir of discontent that remained in the Indian-controlled part of the state after a decade of the insurgency. For a significant segment of the Indian political establishment, the problem in Kashmir was seen either as an expression of recalcitrant Pakistani irredentism or a question of domestic law and order. In fact an astute Indian commentator on Kashmir in a trenchant and candid analysis wrote that:

The patriotic upsurge that swept the whole country during the Kargil conflict did not affect the Kashmir valley. There were no anti-Pakistan demonstrations, no collection campaigns for the welfare of the Kargil jawans, and their families, no expressions of solidarity with them and no blood donation camps. Separatist groups, on the other hand, vied with each other to organize processions in support of the "freedom fighters" of Kargil.[6]

Despite this lack of enthusiasm within Kashmir about the Kargil War, the Indian central (national) government failed to recognize that resentment toward the Indian state had not ended in Kashmir. Indeed it could be argued that unless political turmoil emerged in the state New Delhi would remain content with local governments pursuing routine tasks of governance without urging them to address underlying grievances. This strategy, as this chapter will demonstrate, has proven to be a fundamentally flawed approach and has prevented the country from fashioning a set of policies that could address deep-seated sources of discontent. Indeed, unless such recognition dawns, there is every likelihood that troubles in Kashmir will remain endemic and will periodically erupt. When

5 On the significance of the coup see Sumit Ganguly, "Pakistan's Never-Ending Story: Why the October Coup Was No Surprise," *Foreign Affairs* 79, no. 2 (March/April 2000): 2–9.
6 Balraj Puri, "The Post-Kargil Scene in Kashmir," *The Hindustan Times*, September 10, 1999.

such disturbances ensue, Pakistan, which remains an unrequited party to the dispute, will inevitably seek to foment further discord and stoke the existing sources of discontent. As tensions and disturbances mount, New Delhi will again be induced to resort to force to stop disorder from spreading and thereby reinforce existing antipathy toward the Indian state.

Sadly, even a natural disaster, in the form of a major flood, which devastated significant portions of the Kashmir Valley and especially the winter capital of the state, Srinagar, in September 2014 again brought to the fore the distrust, hostility and alienation of much of the population from the Indian state. Their anger and resentment proved to be especially great because Indian state authorities, overwhelmed with the magnitude of the calamity, proved incapable of coping with the needs of the population.[7]

IN THE AFTERMATH OF KARGIL

The Kargil War had barely come to a close when another major incident rocked an already fragile Indo-Pakistani relationship. This came about as a consequence of the hijacking of an Indian Airlines Airbus to Kandahar, Afghanistan on a routine flight from Kathmandu, Nepal to Lucknow. News of the hijacking came on the late afternoon of December 24, 1999. The hijackers had initially sought to fly the aircraft to Lahore but were denied permission to land. Faced with this refusal they flew the aircraft to Amritsar. Before Indian authorities could attempt a hostage rescue mission the aircraft, with diminishing fuel supplies, nevertheless flew across the border and landed in Lahore. According to a former senior Indian intelligence official, India's lack of preparedness to deal with a possible contingency of this magnitude became apparent at Lahore. If any prior planning had taken place, the runway could have been blocked and the forces from Punjab's Special Operations Group could have been used to storm the plane.[8]

7 Annie Gowen, "Anger Rises in India's Kashmir Valley as People Remain Trapped a Week After Floods," *Washington Post*, September 16, 2014.
8 Personal interview with former senior Indian intelligence official, New Delhi, October 2010.

In Lahore, faced with a lack of cooperation from the Pakistani authorities, it flew to Dubai. In Dubai, the hijackers discarded the body of an Indian passenger whom they had killed.[9] From there the aircraft was flown to Kandahar. After protracted negotiations with Indian interlocutors, which saw the release of three terrorists who had been incarcerated in India, Maulana Masood Azhar, Mushtaq Amhed Zarg and Ahmed Umar Syed,[10] as well as the mortal remains of a Harkat-ul-Ansar operative, Sajjad Afghani, who had been captured and killed in Kashmir, the 150-plus passengers were released.[11]

Two aspects of the hijacking and its aftermath require comment. The first, of course, was the possibility of Pakistan's formal involvement in the episode.[12] If Pakistan was involved, then the question of malign intentions could, yet again, be underscored. Was the Pakistani state complicit? There is little question, based upon US intelligence reports, that elements of the Pakistani security apparatus had acted in concert with the Harkat-ul-Ansar, the group that had plotted and carried out the hijacking. However, what remained unclear were the scope and the extent of such involvement.[13]

The second, of lesser significance, but nevertheless important, was India's handling of the crisis. As a noted Indian journalist commented at the time of the hijacking, the clumsy and uncoordinated handling of the crisis underscored India's limited capacity for crisis management and its obvious unpreparedness to deal with a contingency of this order.[14] Whether or not the Pakistani state was fully

---

9 Suzanne Goldenberg, "Hijackers Given Ultimatum; One Life for 160 Hostage-Takers Say Passengers Go Free if India Releases Cleric Azhar," *Guardian*, December 27, 1999.

10 It is pertinent to mention that Ahmed Umar Syed would later acquire greater notoriety in the killing of the *Wall Street Journal* reporter, Daniel Pearl. See Andrew Buncombe, "A Friend's Labour of Love Reveals Who Killed Daniel Pearl," *Independent*, January 21, 2011.

11 Amit Baruah, "Warning Signals," *Frontline*, 17:1, January 8–21, 2000.

12 Views differ on the question of Pakistan's involvement. For the official view of the United States at the time of the hijacking see Jane Perlez, "Pakistanis Lost Control Of Militants, U.S. Hints," *New York Times*, January 26, 2000.

13 Jane Perlez, "US Says Pakistan Backed Hijackers of Indian Aircraft," *New York Times*, January 25, 2000.

14 Praveen Swami, "Bowing to Terrorism," *Frontline*, 17:1, January 8–21, 2000, pp. 4–9.

complicit in the hijacking, India's obvious vulnerability to a terror-ist plot demonstrated that an adversary could easily exploit extant weaknesses in the country's security apparatus.[15] Unfortunately, these shortcomings were not addressed. Many of them, in fact, came to the fore when operatives of the LeT attacked a set of tar-gets in Bombay (Mumbai) in November 2008 and with devastating consequences.

In the wake of this affair, which again led to a further deterioration in Indo-Pakistani relations, some desultory discussion ensued between the BJP-led government in New Delhi and the National Conference government of Farooq Abdullah in Srinagar on the fraught question of autonomy for the state within the Indian Union.[16] The chief minis-ter, however, was at pains to emphasize that the demands for auton-omy did not constitute a first step toward secession and nor, for that matter, did he envisage a return to the state's pre-1953 status under his father, Sheikh Mohammed Abdullah.[17]

It is unclear if these negotiations or other calculations prompted the most powerful, indigenous militant organization within the state, the HuM, to offer a ceasefire in late July 2000.[18] Some accounts suggested that the United States may have exerted pressure on both the governments of India and Pakistan to try and forge a ceasefire with the HuM.[19] The ceasefire, unfortu-nately, had unintended, perverse consequences. Within a month thereof, elements of the LeT launched a set of vicious attacks in Pahalgam, the base camp of the pilgrims who travel every year to the Amarnath temple, and also in a village in south Kashmir.[20] Despite this attack, the government reiterated its commitment to the ceasefire.[21]

15  Amit Baruah, "Terror Links," *Frontline*, 17:2, January 22–February 4, 2000.
16  Muzamil Jaleel and Nazir Masoodi, "JK Assembly Passes Autonomy Resolution," *The Indian Express*, June 27, 2000.
17  Special Correspondent, "No Fresh Proposals on Autonomy," *The Hindu*, July 21, 2000.
18  Celia W. Dugger, "Rebel Cease-Fire May Signal an Easing of Tensions in Kashmir," *New York Times*, July 31, 2000.
19  Shujaat Bukhari, "Hizbul Announces 'Ceasefire'," *The Hindu*, July 25, 2000; also see Murali Krishnan, "A Quest for Calm," *Outlook*, August 7, 2000.
20  Shujaat Bukhari, "Massacres Rattle Kashmir," *The Hindu*, August 3, 2000.
21  Harish Khare, "Govt. Shaken but Peace Efforts to Continue," *The Hindu*, August 3, 2000.

THE AGRA SUMMIT

Why did Prime Minister Atal Behari Vajpayee, after his deep sense of betrayal in the aftermath of the Kargil War and the terrorist attacks of the summer of 2000, nevertheless agree to the possibility of a summit with General Musharraf in the summer of 2001? The motivations underlying his decision to host Musharraf are far from trivial and instead go to the very basis of this analysis. Was Vajpayee's gesture to Musharraf a sincere attempt to try and embark on a process of reconciliation even after the failure of the Lahore Summit?[22]

There are no clear-cut answers to these questions. The most reliable account suggests that the initiative, in all likelihood, came from the Indian Minister of Home Affairs, L.K. Advani. Apparently, he and some other Cabinet colleagues believed that a "bold and dramatic" gesture might break the existing logjam in Indo-Pakistani relations. Vajpayee, though initially skeptical, accepted this suggestion and invited Musharraf, on May 24.[23]

What is known, however, is that the two sides, despite an apparent air of goodwill, started with very different expectations. Pakistan, from the outset, wanted to focus on the Kashmir dispute. India, on the other hand, wanted a broader dialogue on a range of issues. For India, the items that it deemed most important included Pakistan's support for terror, trade, the reduction of nuclear tensions and attempts to curb drug trafficking.[24] To that end, shortly before the onset of the summit, it had announced a series of CBMs, which included the lowering of tariffs on a range of Pakistani goods, the release of a number of Pakistanis from Indian jails and the easing of some visa and travel restrictions.[25]

The talks started on a somewhat promising note despite the stated differences in the positions of the two sides. In a public statement, Musharraf announced at the outset that he had come to New

---

22  The precise origins of the meeting remain uncertain. For a critical discussion see A.G. Noorani, "The Truth about Agra," *Frontline*, 22:15, July 16–29, 2005.

23  J.N. Dixit, *India-Pakistan in War and Peace* (New Delhi: Books Today, 2002), p. 396.

24  Beth Duff-Brown, "India, Pakistan Talk Peace Sunday," *Contra Costa Times*, July 14, 2001.

25  Nirmal Ghosh, "Pragmatism Essential to India-Pakistan Détente," *The Straits Times*, July 11, 2001.

Delhi "with an open mind."[26] Despite this seemingly positive out-look Musharraf's decision to meet with members of the Kashmiri separatist APHC at a reception at the Pakistan High Commission in New Delhi irked his Indian hosts.[27]

This issue notwithstanding, the formal talks appeared to make progress when Musharraf met Vajpayee for nearly an hour and a half for a one-on-one discussion. Specifically, according to some reports the two parties had discussed a formula under which they would address the Kashmir issue with each making some conces-sions.[28] Hopes of an understanding however quickly ended in an impasse over Pakistan's single-minded focus on the Kashmir dis-pute and India's insistence that the question of cross-border terror-ism be also addressed forthrightly.[29]

Why did the talks end in a deadlock? According to key individ-uals who were involved in the discussions two factors in particular led to the standoff. An Indian Foreign Service officer, who played a vital role in the discussions, claimed that the talks unraveled because Musharraf had come to the summit with a completely exaggerated sense of what could be accomplished in a single meeting. It is not clear precisely what he had hoped to achieve but it was evident that he wanted to demonstrate some tangible progress toward a reso-lution of the Kashmir dispute.[30] Additionally, a key intelligence offi-cial, who was also present at the meeting, argues that the Minister of Home Affairs, L.K. Advani, had adamantly insisted that no agree-ment was possible unless the issue of Pakistan's support for terror was forthrightly addressed in any final communiqué or agreement. Interesting enough, he also claims that both the Indian Minister for External Affairs, Jaswant Singh, and Prime Minister Vajpayee had

---

26  Agence France Presse, "India and Pakistan Agree to Look Forward at Summit," July 14, 2001.
27  Luke Harding, "Kashmir Clashes Cast Cloud Over Delhi Summit," *Observer*, July 15, 2001.
28  Nirmal Ghosh, "India-Pakistan Summit Gets Off to a Good Start," *The Straits Times*, July 16, 2001; also see Celia W. Dugger, "India-Pakistan Talks: Many Hopes, No Details," *New York Times*, July 16, 2001.
29  Harbaksh Singh Nanda, "India, Pakistan Talks End in Deadlock," *United Press International*, July 16, 2001.
30  Personal interview with retired senior Indian Foreign Service officer, December 15, 2012, New Delhi.

been willing to grant Musharraf leeway on the Kashmir question without an insistence on the inclusion of the matter of Pakistan's involvement with terror.[31]

The failure of the summit, for all practical purposes, put the dialogue in cold storage.[32] The inability to make any headway with Pakistan at this meeting made it politically untenable for the Vajpayee regime to continue any viable discussions with Pakistan.[33] Simultaneously, Musharraf, after having shed his uniform and traveled to New Delhi, but without any tangible outcomes, evinced no interest in following up on the discussions.

Despite this stalemate, some hopes were raised about a Musharraf–Vajpayee meeting in New York during the annual session of the United Nations General Assembly in September. However, the Al Qaeda terrorist attacks on the United States on September 11, 2001 effectively undermined any hopes for such a meeting. To compound matters, the United States promptly turned to Pakistan following its decision to topple the Taliban regime in Afghanistan, where it believed that the attacks had originated. Worse still, key American decision-makers, and especially Richard Armitage, the US Deputy Secretary of State, believed that India's offer of assistance was simply a crude attempt to marginalize Pakistan at this moment of crisis.[34] Pakistan's willingness to assist the United States, of course, from the outset was qualified. This limited support for American objectives emerged even as it acceded to seven American demands. They were to stop Al Qaeda operatives at the border, provide the United States with blanket landing rights to conduct operations, to provide territorial and naval access to the United States, to share intelligence, to publicly condemn terrorist attacks, cut off recruits and supplies to the Taliban, break off diplomatic ties with the Taliban and to help locate Osama bin Laden.[35] In the end, however, it would help the United States to attack Al Qaeda targets but

31 Interview with former senior Indian intelligence official, New Delhi, October 2010.
32 C. Raja Mohan, "Agra Talks Fail," *The Hindu*, July 17, 2001.
33 Shishir Gupta, "Dialogue Dilemma," *India Today*, September 3, 2001.
34 Interview with retired senior US Foreign Service Officer, Washington, DC, July 2014.
35 Agencies, "Musharraf Accepted Seven US Demands in 24 Hours After 9/11 Terror Attacks," *The Economic Times*, September 17, 2010.

would not end its support for the Kashmiri insurgents, or for that matter, elements of the Taliban.[36]

Indian interlocutors realized that revamping the discussions with Pakistan would be difficult, given US–Pakistan cooperation in the war against Al Qaeda. Instead they sought to make common cause with the Bush administration. To that end, they unsuccessfully sought to link Pakistan's support for terror in Kashmir with the administration's "global war against terror."

Throughout the fall of 2001 there were occasional efforts to renew the dialogue while various incidents along the LoC in Kashmir continued to vitiate the atmosphere. As the possibilities of the resumption of a dialogue remained in abeyance an unprecedented and brazen terrorist attack on the Indian parliament, on December 13, 2001, for all practical purposes ended all such efforts. Indeed the terrorist attack on the Indian parliament, and its antecedents, again underscored that the Pakistani military's unremitting hostility toward India had remained unaltered. Chapter 4 will discuss the attack and its aftermath.

---

36 Phillip J. Quinlan, "Pakistan: A Conflicted Ally in the Fight Against Terrorism Since 9/11," *Global Security Studies* 3, no. 1 (Winter 2012): 1–14.

# 4

# The road to Operation Parakram

Chapter 2 explored in some detail how the Kargil conflict had undermined the limited trust that the Lahore peace process had engendered. It also showed that the fragmented structure of political authority within Pakistan placed the understandings reached at Lahore in jeopardy. In effect, Nawaz had been incapable of making a "credible commitment" because the military establishment was not in accord with his interest in seeking a rapprochement with India.[1] Subsequently, despite Prime Minister Vajpayee's efforts to continue a dialogue with Pakistan, the Agra Summit fell apart. This time both Musharraf's rigidity on issues pertaining to the Kashmir dispute and the Indian Deputy Prime Minister's Lal Krishna Advani's insistence on the inclusion of language dealing with Pakistan's willingness to end its support for terror contributed to the impasse.

This chapter will examine how, as a consequence of a Pakistan-based terrorist attack, the bilateral relationship took a substantial turn for the worse. Thanks to Pakistan's possession of nuclear weapons, the unavailability of any viable pre-planned conventional military options for a swift and calibrated reprisal, and persistent American diplomatic pressures to refrain from any precipitate military action prevented India from launching a

---

1 On the concept of a "credible commitment" see James D. Fearon, "Rationalist Explanations for War," *International Organization* 49, no. 3 (Summer 1995): 379–414.

conventional attack on Pakistan. Instead it resorted to a strategy of coercive diplomacy to try and induce Pakistan to end its support for terror. As this chapter will show, there were distinct limits to India's ability to induce Pakistan to make any significant commitment to terminate its dalliance with terror.[2] In this context, it is important to reiterate the central argument of this book. The strategic imperatives of the military order in Pakistan made it impervious to external pressures to abandon its intransigence toward India.

It will also argue that Pakistan, under military pressure from India, and diplomatic prodding from the United States, did undertake some measures to curb its support for the use of terror as part of its asymmetric war strategy against India. However, it evinced no willingness to eschew that strategy. Instead it merely curbed the activities of various groups and organizations that it had nurtured and supported to pursue its strategic goals against India.

This leads to the conclusion that it was not India's military acquisitions, force postures or deployment choices that prodded Pakistan to undertake risky proxy war strategies against India. Some Indian military acquisitions and force deployments may have, at best, accelerated and boosted particular Pakistani choices. Even in their absence, however, the Pakistani security establishment was intent on using asymmetric forces against a far more powerful adversary primarily to pursue a long-nurtured set of grievances. In effect, it was most assuredly not a status quo power, but instead one that was committed to addressing its long-standing resentments through the use of proxy forces.

The chapter concludes with a discussion of how, with American diplomatic prodding, the two sides embarked upon a new dialogue that formally commenced in 2004.

### THE CRISIS UNFOLDS: PHASE ONE

Even though parliament was in session in New Delhi on December 13, 2001, security was not in an especially heightened state.

---

2 Sumit Ganguly and Michael R. Kraig, "The 2001–2002 Indo-Pakistani Crisis: Exposing the Limits of Coercive Diplomacy in South Asia," *Security Studies* 14, no. 2 (April–June 2005): 290–324; for a discussion of why

Consequently, when a seemingly ubiquitous white Ambassador car with its obligatory red light on the roof, until recently the preferred vehicle of senior government officials, pulled up at the principal entrance, the parliamentary security guards paid no particular heed to it. Since the car had a Ministry of Home Affairs label, the security personnel allowed it to enter.[3] Within minutes a group of well-armed men emerged from the vehicle and proceeded toward the Central Hall of parliament while unleashing a volley of shots from automatic weapons. Fortunately, an unarmed "watch and ward" guard had the presence of mind to swiftly close the main door and thereby managed to prevent much loss of life.

As the police personnel assigned to parliamentary security duties belatedly recognized their error they swung into action. Over the next several hours the gun battle that ensued led to the deaths of all five terrorists and seven security personnel. Within days, based upon electronic intercepts, the Indian intelligence services concluded that the terrorists were linked to two Pakistan-based organizations, the LeT and the JeM.[4] As the police proceeded to gather more information about the antecedents of the attackers and their support network within India, the BJP-led NDA government embarked on a diplomatic offensive against Pakistan.[5]

the strategy to coerce Pakistan failed see Patrick Bratton, "Signals and Orchestration: India's Use of Compellence in the 2001–02 Crisis," *Strategic Analysis* 34, no. 4 (July 2010): 594–610. Bratton argues that the strategy was unsuccessful because the demands on Pakistan were inconsistent, there was inadequate civil–military coordination and the Indian government put pressure on Pakistan while also prodding the United States to do the same. This final component, he argues, worked at cross-purposes.

3  Purnima S. Tripathi, "Terror in Parliament," *Frontline*, 18:26, December 22, 2001–January 4, 2002.

4  For a useful overview see Nicholas Howenstein, *The Jihadi Terrain in Pakistan: An Introduction to the Sunni Jihadi Groups in Pakistan and Kashmir* (Bradford: University of Bradford, Pakistan Security Research Unit, 2008).

5  Despite angry calls for prompt military action against Pakistan, Indian policy-makers chose to pursue a strategy of coercive diplomacy. As the Indian Minister of External Affairs, Jaswant Singh, later recorded in his memoirs, "What we did adopt was coercive diplomacy, a combination of diplomatic and military pressure." See Jaswant Singh, *A Call to Honour: In Service of Emergent India* (New Delhi: Rupa and Company, 2006), p. 266.

Their diplomatic efforts did produce some results, but these were mostly cosmetic.[6] President Bush chose to place the LeT and the JeM on the US Department of State's Foreign Terrorist Organization list.[7] This action, taken on December 20, ensured the freezing of the financial assets of the two groups, and prevented their members from traveling to the United States. Faced with the American crackdown on these two terrorist groups, General Musharraf moved to shut down their offices in two key Pakistani cities.

However, it needs to be underscored that his actions were mostly superficial and did not really address India's concerns about Pakistan's ongoing support for terror. The commitment to other insurgent groups in Kashmir continued unabated.[8] If Musharraf was genuinely interested in establishing even a modicum of trust with India, his actions certainly belied any such intent. His actions were mostly designed to ward off American and international pressure in the wake of the attacks on the Indian parliament.

Even as Pakistan went through these motions, India recalled its High Commissioner (ambassador) from Pakistan on December 22, broke off all road and rail links and demanded the repatriation of some 20 individuals, several of whom were from Pakistan and had all been charged with acts of terror committed on Indian soil. Soon thereafter, Pakistani civilian aircraft were prohibited from flying over Indian territory and a statement from the Indian Minister of Defense, George Fernandes, indicated that Indian fighter jets had been moved to forward positions.[9]

Simultaneously, India's political leadership approached the Indian military about possible strike options against Pakistan.

6 According to a former senior Indian intelligence official, under the instructions of the Pakistani military, the LeT in particular were told to lay off on attacks on Western targets. Personal interview, New Delhi, October 18, 2010.

7 T.V. Parasuram, "Bush Asks Pak to Act Against LeT, JeM," *The Economic Times*, December 23, 2001; also see David E. Sanger and Kurt Eichenwald, "Citing India Attack, US Aims at Assets of Group in Pakistan," *New York Times*, December 21, 2001.

8 John F. Burns and Celia W. Dugger, "India Builds Up Forces as Bush Urges Calm," *New York Times*, December 30, 2001.

9 See Rajesh Basrur, "Coercive Diplomacy in a Nuclear Environment," in Rafiq Dossani and Henry S. Rowen (eds.), *Prospects for Peace in South Asia* (Stanford: Stanford University Press, 2005).

Given the state of India's readiness and the deployment of its forces, they were informed that a substantial operation that could have significant military consequences for Pakistan would take at least three weeks.[10] Indeed, it was not until January 11, 2002 that Indian forces were in a sufficient state of mobilization to be able to carry out planned operations against Pakistan.[11] The Chief of Staff of the Indian Army in a press conference also made it clear that India was ready for war and would retaliate with nuclear weapons should Pakistan resort to a first use thereof.[12]

Thanks to the elapsed time, Pakistan had ample opportunity to bolster its own capabilities and consequently any element of surprise that India had counted on was effectively lost.[13] To compound matters, on January 12, 2002, under considerable American pressure, General Musharraf gave a public address over national television in Pakistan where he stated that he would not allow Pakistan's territory to be used in the future to carry out acts of terror against any country.[14] More specifically, he banned the Sipah-i-Sahaba Pakistan (Pakistan Army of the Prophet's Companions), Tehrik-i-Jaferia Pakistan (Pakistan's Shia Movement), Tanzim Nifaz-i-Shariat-i-Mohammadi (Organization for the Establishment of the Law of Mohammed) and the Jaish-e-Mohammed (Force of Mohammed). He also instituted new measures for the registration of religious schools, foreign students and teachers and the use of loudspeakers in mosques.[15] Significantly, Musharraf did not act against one of the

10 Discussions with senior Indian military personnel, New Delhi, November 2010.
11 Lt. Gen. V.K. Sood and Pravin Sawhney, *Operation Parakram: The War Unfinished* (New Delhi: Sage Publications, 2003).
12 Celia W. Dugger, "A Blunt Speaking General Says India Is Ready for War," *New York Times*, January 11, 2002.
13 In an interview, the then Chief of Army Staff, General Padmanabhan, admitted as much. See Praveen Swami, "General Padmanabhan Mulls Over Lessons of Operation Parakram," *The Hindu*, February 6, 2004.
14 The choice of his words was quite significant. In alluding to Pakistani territory he had, in fact, excluded Pakistan-controlled Kashmir. Under Pakistani law, those portions of Kashmir under Pakistani control are nominally independent. For a discussion of its status under international law see Navnita Chadha Behera, *Demystifying Kashmir* (Washington, DC: The Brookings Institution, 2006).
15 Ian Talbot, "Pakistan in 2002: Democracy, Terrorism, and Brinkmanship," *Asian Survey* 43, no. 1 (January/February 2003): 198–207.

most important terrorist organizations operating within Kashmir, the Hizb-ul-Mujahideen ("Party of holy warriors").[16]

His public disavowal of continuing support for terror made it exceedingly difficult for India's political leadership to carry out any military action against Pakistan.[17] Given the dilemma that it confronted, India's policy-makers chose to pursue a strategy of forceful persuasion against Pakistan to dismantle what they referred to as its "infrastructure of terror" and also to comply with India's initial demands.

To that end, India's policy-makers debated the possible military options available to them. Initially there was much public clamor for air strikes against terrorist camps located in Pakistan. However, as early as December 17, the Indian service chiefs argued before the apex CCS that such strikes would be of limited efficacy in blunting the terrorist threats. These camps, which apparently amounted to little more than "drill squares and firing ranges," could be easily reconstituted. Furthermore, such attacks were fraught with the prospect of military escalation.[18]

The strategy that was eventually adopted involved the swift deployment of a substantial portion of the Indian Army along India's western border with Pakistan, with the goal of inducing Pakistan to comply with India's demands. Indeed the Pakistani military considered the Indian mobilization to be unprecedented. It was the first time that troops from India's Eastern Command were mobilized and moved to the western sector to deal with a contingency involving Pakistan. Furthermore, mines were laid along the LoC and also along the international border with Pakistan. Simultaneously, theIAF was placed on full alert status.

Over the next several months, tensions steadily mounted in the subcontinent. The George W. Bush administration, which was acutely concerned about the prosecution of the war in Afghanistan against the remnants of the Taliban and Al Qaeda, stepped up its diplomatic

---

16  Owen Bennett Jones, "Musharraf's Kashmir Policy," *Asian Affairs* 38, no. 3 (November 2007): 305–317.

17  Personal Interview with a former Indian National Security Adviser, New Delhi, June 2008.

18  S. Kalyanaraman, "Operation Parakram: An Indian Exercise in Coercive Diplomacy," *Strategic Analysis* 26, no. 4 (2002): 478–492.

efforts in South Asia. To that end, it sent out a series of Cabinet level officials at various junctures in efforts to hobble the possibilities of an Indo-Pakistani conflict. It feared that a worsening of the Indo-Pakistani conflict would invariably distract Pakistan's attention away from supporting the American military efforts in Afghanistan.

## PHASE TWO

There is little question that concerted US diplomacy during this crisis did stay India's hand. However, there is also considerable evidence that in the wake of a second attack at a military base at Kaluchak in Indian-controlled Kashmir on May 14, 2002, killing several children and wives of Indian Army personnel, India considered military action against Pakistan. Indeed, following this attack the prospect of an Indian attack on Pakistan seemed imminent.[19] Prime Minister Vajpayee's harsh public statements reflected Indian frustrations with Pakistan's inability or unwillingness to rein in various terrorist entities.[20] Simultaneously, the Chief of Staff of the Indian Army, General Sundarajan Padmanabhan, stated "the time for action has come."[21]

Nevertheless, despite this public display of anger, India chose not to resort to force. Indeed, India's failure to at least undertake token strikes against targets across the LoC in Kashmir, if not into Pakistani territory, appears puzzling. Since Indian military capabilities were on alert and deployed at strategic salients, the failure to carry out any punitive actions appears all the more curious.

There are only three plausible explanations that can be adduced to explain Indian inaction after the Kaluchak massacre. One may well have been the fear of escalation given that Pakistani units were obviously in a state of readiness as the crisis was now well into its fifth month.[22] A second possible reason may have been prompt American

---

19  Praveen Swami, "Building Confrontation," *Frontline*, 19:11, May 25–June 7, 2002.
20  Atul Aneja and Sandeep Dikshit, "There is National Anger, Vajpayee Tells Blair," *The Hindu*, May 28, 2002.
21  Edward Luce, "India Prepares for Strike on Camps," *Financial Times*, May 17, 2002.
22  It is pertinent to note that this attack took place as Christina Rocca, the Assistant Secretary of State for South Asia, was in New Delhi in an effort to

pressure calling for restraint.[23] A third reason, which was present throughout the entire crisis, was the risk of nuclear escalation.[24]

To compound matters, as the nation was still reeling from the shock of the Kaluchak massacre, on May 21 Abdul Ghani Lone, a moderate Kashmiri leader of long standing, was assassinated.[25] Once again, Pakistan formally condemned his killing. However, in the wake of his death, the Indian political establishment concluded that it was a clear signal from the terrorists operating in Kashmir that any leader of consequence who sought a negotiated settlement of the Kashmir dispute was at considerable personal risk. Shortly after Abdul Ghani Lone's death, on May 27, Musharraf gave yet another public address where he again reaffirmed his willingness to end infiltration into Kashmir.[26]

Despite his reaffirmation, the Bush administration felt compelled to intervene in the ongoing crisis. In all likelihood the administration chose to pursue high-level diplomacy because India's actions were starting to mirror its public rhetoric. For example, the IAF moved several squadrons of fighter aircraft to forward military bases, the navy moved five of its most sophisticated vessels from the eastern to the western fleet and its only operational aircraft carrier, INS *Viraat*, was taken out of dry dock and placed on alert near the coast of Bombay (Mumbai).[27] Tensions were also at an all-time high along the LoC in Kashmir, as both Indian and Pakistani troops remained in a high state of alert and prepared for the possibility of

defuse the ongoing tensions. See Sumit Ganguly and R. Harrison Wagner, "India and Pakistan: Bargaining in the Shadow of Nuclear War," *The Journal of Strategic Studies* 27, no. 3 (September 2004): 479–507.

23 Josy Joseph, "Jammu Attack Ruins Rocca's Peace Mission," *India Abroad*, May 24, 2002.

24 According to a former Chief of Staff of the Indian Army, two factors explain India's restraint in the wake of the Kaluchak massacre. First, there was significant American diplomatic pressure on the NDA regime calling for restraint. Second, the fear of nuclear escalation though not discussed in much detail in decision-making circles, cast a shadow over all deliberations. Personal interview with former Chief of Staff, Indian Army, December 14, 2010.

25 Basharat Peer, "'Moderate' Separatist Leader Abdul Ghani Lone Murdered," *India Abroad*, May 31, 2002.

26 See the discussion of Indian responses to Musharraf's speech in Alex Stolar, *To The Brink: Indian Decision-Making and the 2001–2002 Standoff* (Washington, DC: The Henry L. Stimson Center, 2008).

27 Josy Joseph, "The Mood is for War," *India Abroad*, May 31, 2002.

war.[28] What really focused the attention of the Bush administration, however, was Pakistan's tests of three nuclear-capable missiles within the span of a week in May.[29]

To that end, it dispatched the Deputy Secretary of State, Richard Armitage, and then Secretary of Defense, Donald Rumsfeld, to both Islamabad and New Delhi. In Islamabad, they told the Pakistani regime that infiltration into Kashmir had to come to a close, and in New Delhi they sought a drawing down of Indian forces along the Indo-Pakistani border.[30] In the wake of these visits the crisis wound down as both Indian and Pakistani forces started phased withdrawals from their forward deployments. However, the risks of a conflict nevertheless remained quite high.[31]

Why did India not resort to force against Pakistan in the immediate aftermath of the initial terrorist attack on December 13, 2001? What did Operation Parakram accomplish? There is a clear-cut answer to the first question. Apparently, the military managed to achieve basic mobilization within the first 48 hours of the attack. However, the actual ability to strike Pakistan in a fashion that would have caused significant damage apparently took at least two weeks. By then, of course, any element of surprise was wholly lost.[32]

Some Indian analysts have argued that it achieved its goals because Pakistan-sponsored terrorism tapered off in the fall of

28 Dexter Filkins, "On Kashmir Line, Pakistanis Wait, With Few Illusions," *New York Times*, June 2, 2002.

29 See Alex Wagner, "Pakistan Tests Three Nuclear-Capable Ballistic Missiles," *Arms Control Today*, June 1, 2002. Available at: www.armscontrol.org/act/2002_06/paktestjune02.

30 For a discussion of the American role in defusing this crisis see Mary Anne Weaver, *Pakistan: In the Shadow of Jihad and Afghanistan* (New York: Farrar, Straus and Giroux, 2002); also see Josy Joseph, "Armitage Sees Lessening of Tension," *India Abroad*, June 14, 2002.

31 Sadanand Dhume and Joanna Slater, "Tension Down, Danger High," *Far Eastern Economic Review*, June 20, 2003.

32 Personal interview with former Chief of Staff of the Indian Army, New Delhi, December 14, 2010. It is worth noting that India had no viable military options that it could exercise promptly in the wake of the attack because a number of key Indian decision-makers had argued quite vigorously in the wake of the Kargil War that India could fight a limited conventional war under the nuclear umbrella. General Ved Prakash Malik, who was the Chief of Staff of the Indian Army at the time of the Kargil conflict, was one of the most vocal exponents of this position. On this subject see General V.P. Malik, "The Lessons of Kargil,"

2002. They also argue that it was successful as it made the global community aware of Pakistan's involvement with terror.[33] Others, however, argue that the Indian strategy of coercive diplomacy failed to accomplish most of the stated objectives.[34]

Indian anxieties about resurgent tensions remained alive because of a number of compelling reasons. Pakistan's past behavior gave India's policy-makers little reason to believe that the drop in infiltration in Kashmir was necessarily permanent. Additionally, they had their doubts about whether or not Pakistan would actually move to rein in the various terrorist organizations that it had spawned over many years. Finally, they remained concerned about the possibility of Pakistan's security establishment aiming to disrupt the upcoming elections in Jammu and Kashmir scheduled for October 2002.[35] To sum up, the cognitive predispositions of the Indian leadership, based upon their prior experiences of dealing with Pakistan, had made them wary about accepting this stated commitment to end infiltration at face value.[36] In the event, the elections proved to be remarkably successful despite the looming threat of terror, though the ruling party of long standing, the Jammu and Kashmir National Conference, suffered a critical blow.[37]

IN THE AFTERMATH OF THE CRISIS

It is doubtful that any positive structural change in Indo-Pakistani relations emerged from India's exercise of coercive diplomacy in the

www.bharat-rakshak.com/MONITOR/ISSUE4-6/malik.html (accessed on May 13, 2011); also see the thoughtful critique of this argument in Rajesh M. Basrur, "Kargil, Terrorism, and India's Strategic Shift," *India Review* 1, no. 4 (October 2002): 39–56.

33  Personal Interview with senior Indian security correspondent, New Delhi, December 2002.
34  Ganguly and Kraig, 2005; also see Josy Joseph, "Exercise in Futility," *India Abroad*, December 27, 2002.
35  Gaurav Kampani, "The Indo-Pakistani Military Standoff: Why It is Not Over Yet," *India Abroad*, July 19, 2002.
36  For a discussion of cognitive processes in decision-making see Yaacov Y.I. Vertzberger, *The World in Their Minds: Information Processing, Cognition, and Perception in Foreign Policy Decisionmaking* (Palo Alto: Stanford University Press, 1990).
37  Amy Waldman, "Ruling Kashmir Party Suffers Severe Setback at Polls," *New York Times*, October 11, 2002.

2001–2 crisis. At best, infiltration from Pakistan may have tapered off somewhat. However, President Musharraf and the military remained firmly ensconced in power, no serious efforts were undertaken to dismantle the network of terrorist organizations based in and operating from Pakistani soil, and the regime made no further commitments toward rapprochement with India.

Despite this lugubrious outcome, the Vajpayee regime persisted in its efforts to re-open a dialogue with Pakistan. In May 2003, Vajpayee again reiterated his interest in renewing the dialogue with Pakistan. Once again, the choice of the venue for this announcement was quite significant. It was a public rally held at the Sher-e-Kashmir cricket stadium in Srinagar, the capital of the Indian-controlled portion of the disputed state of Jammu and Kashmir. This was the first time in 15 years that an Indian prime minister had appeared at a major public gathering in the city.

Some observers argued that Vajpayee had chosen to make this announcement to pre-empt any possible American pressure to resume a dialogue with Pakistan.[38] Furthermore, others argued that Vajpayee had also chosen to take advantage of improved conditions within the state of Jammu and Kashmir, which had recently witnessed its first free and fair local election in October 2002, the first in several years. Offering to hold talks with Pakistan could enable his regime to consolidate the political gains that had been made in the state. Though he had both external and internal incentives to renew discussions with Pakistan, his decision to act was not without potential domestic political risks and costs. Many individuals and some factions within his party remained hostile to any prospect of reconciliation with Pakistan because of its failure or unwillingness to end the support for terror.[39]

In fact, the issue of continuing terrorism was much on their minds as Richard Armitage was scheduled to visit New Delhi and Islamabad in May following an earlier visit of the Indian National Security Adviser, Brajesh Mishra, to Washington, DC.[40] In the wake

38  V. Sudarshan, "Over the Boundary at Sher-E-Kashmir," *Outlook*, May 12, 2003.
39  Amy Waldman, "India Announces Steps in Effort to End Its Conflict With Pakistan," *New York Times*, May 3, 2003.
40  C. Raja Mohan, "Armitage to Visit India, Pak. Next Month," *The Hindu*. April 18, 2003.

of Armitage's mission to India and Pakistan, reports emerged in the Indian press that Pakistan was undertaking small but significant steps to rein in anti-Indian jihadi forces.[41]

This reduction in infiltration was probably linked to a realization on Musharraf's part that the strategy of dislodging India from the portion of Kashmir that it had long controlled was not a viable strategy. Apparently, he had consulted several of his senior generals and they had collectively concluded that Pakistan could not sustain its military expenditures in the absence of economic growth. Such growth, in turn, was predicated on peace with India.[42] Accordingly, in November 2003 he announced a unilateral ceasefire along the LoC. India promptly reciprocated and the artillery barrages came to a close. Before long the two sides worked out other CBMs. Soon thereafter Musharraf demonstrated greater flexibility about possible negotiations when he publicly stated that he was willing to set aside the United Nations Resolutions of 1948 and 1949 on Kashmir in the quest for a settlement of the dispute with India.[43]

This was a dramatic concession on his part. However, it is far from clear that he enjoyed significant domestic support, especially within the crucial constituency of the Army, on this issue. Internal backing for such an initiative would need to extend beyond the confines of the security establishment alone. Their willingness to agree to such a dramatic shift in the country's passionately held stance would constitute a dramatic departure. However, even beyond their consent the long history of Pakistan's past commitment to the implementation of these resolutions would require any leader to forge a wider domestic political consensus to actually abandon the plebiscite option. The resolutions, as is well known, had called for the holding of a plebiscite to determine the wishes of the Kashmiris about possible accession to either India or Pakistan.

---

41  B. Muralidhar Reddy, "Militant Groups in PoK Asked to 'Close Camps'," *The Hindu*, May 31, 2003; also see B. Muralidhar Reddy, "Expectations and Some Worries," *Frontline*, 20:12, June 7–20, 2003.
42  Steve Coll, "The Back Channel," *The New Yorker*, March 2, 2009.
43  "Pakistan, India Need to be Bold on Kashmir: UN Resolutions can be 'Set Aside': Musharraf," *Dawn*, December 19, 2003.

## THE ORIGINS AND EVOLUTION OF COLD START

Despite the willingness of the Vajpayee regime to seek a pathway to rapprochement with Pakistan, the Indian defense community continued its quest to fashion a military strategy to cope with Pakistan's unwillingness to abandon the jihadi option. This endeavor, of course, had its origins in the discussions of limited war under the nuclear umbrella in the aftermath of the Kargil crisis. The long, costly and ultimately largely futile military deployment that India had undertaken in the wake of the December 13 attack on parliament had clearly underscored the limits of such a strategy of coercive diplomacy. The inability of India's armed forces to quickly mobilize and carry out effective punitive strikes against specific targets in Pakistan had been laid bare in the days and weeks of the onset of the crisis. This new doctrine was now designed to ensure that the country's policy-makers would not again find themselves so hobbled.

Despite the interest in devising a doctrine and strategy to respond to Pakistani provocations, the Indian military establishment faced important structural and organizational hurdles in pursuit of these ends. Two important analyses of the doctrine have highlighted these shortcomings.[44] However, before summarizing the key findings of these two analyses, it is important to spell out the key features of this proposed new doctrine.

It calls for the transformation of force structure, it emphasizes speed, focuses on limited objectives and requires a combined arms operation. In terms of force structure the large "strike corps" will be broken up into eight, forward deployed, division-sized "integrated battle groups" (IBGs). Speed will also characterize this new strategy and there will be an emphasis on both rapid mobilization and swift maneuver. It will also have limited objectives avoiding deep penetration of Pakistani territory. Finally, it will attempt to coordinate the actions of the Air Force and the Navy in concert with the Army's ground actions.[45]

---

44 Walter C. Ladwig III, "A Cold Start to Hot Wars? The Indian Army's New Limited War Doctrine," *International Security* 32, no. 3 (Winter 2007/8): 158–190 and Shashank Joshi, "India's Military Instrument: A Doctrine Still Born," *Journal of Strategic Studies* 36, no. 4 (2013): 512–540.

45 For a thoughtful Pakistani response to India's pursuit of this new doctrine see Air Commodore Tariq M. Ashraf, "Doctrinal Reawakening of the Indian Armed Forces," *Military Review* (November–December 2004): 53–62.

These ambitious plans and goals face a number of important constraints. One analyst has identified at least five such hurdles. They are the role of nuclear weapons, the escalatory potential of the limited war doctrine and the consequent unwillingness of civilian authority to embrace it, the persistence of inter-services rivalry, the lack of readiness to take on a task of this magnitude and the onus of these new military tactics. Each of these requires brief discussion.

The Pakistani possession of nuclear weapons and its stated willingness to resort to their use when faced with an Indian incursion of any magnitude into Pakistani territory significantly complicates India's war plans.[46] Furthermore, Pakistan's acquisition of a particular nuclear-capable ballistic missile of extremely short range might be a possible indicator of a design to thwart Indian plans of making a swift, sharp but limited grab of Pakistani territory.[47] Apart from Pakistan's possible low nuclear threshold, India's political elite has not displayed much propensity for risk proneness in recent conflicts. Indeed some analysts have argued that there is an Indian proclivity for strategic restraint.[48] Consequently, it is not entirely clear that even if the doctrine were enacted, Indian civilian authorities would grant the military the necessary leeway to implement it. To compound matters, as a number of observers have argued, inter-services rivalry continues to plague decision-making in India. Unfortunately, despite decades of desultory discussions little progress has been made in resolving these differences. Given their persistence it remains unclear that the three services would be able to act in concert to implement this new doctrine.[49] Even if the problems of inter-service coordination could be overcome, the sheer scope and dimensions of this new strategy are daunting. Apparently even in the aftermath of the Bombay (Mumbai) terrorist attacks

46  Peter R. Lavoy, "Pakistan's Nuclear Doctrine," in Dossani and Rowen, 2005.
47  Global Security Newswire Staff, "Pakistan Seen Readying to Cross Nuclear Threshold," *The Atlantic*, June 2, 2011. Available at: www.theatlantic.com/international/archive/2011/06/pakistan-seen-readying-to-cross-nuclear-threshold/239817/.
48  See for example, Stephen P. Cohen and Sunil Dasgupta, *Arming Without Aiming: India's Military Modernization* (Washington, DC: The Brookings Institution, 2010).
49  Kalyan Ray, "Inter-Service Rivalry Draws Antony's Ire," *The Deccan Herald*, February 28, 2012.

the army would have required several weeks to undertaken a viable operation against Pakistan. Finally, the Army faces a demanding task of how to carry out this new doctrine when already tied down in the Himalayas against an increasingly restive PLA.[50] Given all these structural and situational constraints the effectiveness of this new doctrine really remains in question.[51]

Indeed an earlier and careful analysis of the Indian Army's recent exercises designed to test the viability of the Cold Start strategy provided a distinctly mixed picture of the capabilities and readiness of the military to accomplish the stated goals. The assessment revealed that though the relevant units performed with some skill and dexterity in the exercises they nevertheless needed several days or longer of rehearsals to be able to carry out the assigned tasks. Furthermore, an issue that seems to still plague Indian defense planners, namely the question of joint operations, was found lacking in a series of exercises. Apparently despite multiple rehearsals, the Army and the Air Force failed to demonstrate the kind of integration that an operation of the order envisaged. Despite these shortcomings, the same evaluation also revealed that the Indian military had made significant progress in the use of advanced information technology and communications systems in battlefield conditions. Finally, this analysis also underscored the long-standing problems of inter-service rivalry and civil–military relations. Neither of the latter two issues, unfortunately, is amenable to quick resolution.[52]

Beyond these considerations other issues are also likely to hobble the implementation of the Cold Start doctrine as an operational strategy. The poor quality of India's road and rail networks are likely to constrain the rapid movement of armor formations as quickly as desired. Furthermore, even if such mobility were available Pakistan could strike and degrade the networks through the use of long-range missiles. Additionally, over the course of the past decade Pakistan has started to put in place its own countermeasures to thwart Cold Start. Specifically, it has moved various armor formations closer

50 Jeff M. Smith, "Sino-Indian Relations: A Troubled History, An Uncertain Future," *Harvard International Review* 33, no. 1 (Spring 2011).

51 Much of this description and analysis has been drawn from Joshi, 2013.

52 Much of this description and analysis has been drawn from Ladwig, 2007/8.

to the intended areas of operations, dumped ammunition and fuel closer to those areas, has improved coordination with the PAF and has also developed its own ground doctrine. More to the point, it has rehearsed possible scenarios under the aegis of a series of exercises entitled Azm-e-Nau.[53]

Though the Indian military establishment sought to devise a working strategy to deal with Pakistan's asymmetric war strategy, India's political leadership did not abandon its quest to reach a rapprochement with Pakistan. The quest for a proactive military strategy while pursuing a diplomatic strategy to ease tensions with Pakistan might suggest a disjuncture in policy coordination. However, it may not necessarily reflect a policy dissensus. From an Indian politico-military standpoint, the pursuit of a quick reaction military doctrine may well have seemed compatible with the continuing effort to reduce strains with Pakistan using diplomatic means. That said, from the standpoint of the Pakistani security establishment, India's quest for a military doctrine that was focused on prompt conventional retaliation against what it believed was a Pakistan-sponsored terrorist attack, contributed to spiral dynamics. Evidence for this process can be gleaned from important Pakistani statements on the subject.[54]

In part, this stemmed from General Musharraf's stated willingness to renew a dialogue process. According to an informed analyst of Pakistan's domestic and international politics Musharraf's willingness to restore negotiations with India stemmed from growing domestic turmoil and the military's weariness with confrontation with India over a span of two years.[55] What remains, unclear, however, is if his willingness to restart a dialogue with India was merely to give Pakistan a reprieve or if it reflected a shift in his policy priorities.

Musharraf's task was made easier, because in April 2003 Prime Minister Vajpayee, while on a visit to Srinagar, had made a public speech calling for restarting the dialogue. The precise motivations underlying Vajpayee's decision to extend this "hand of friendship"

---

53  Personal correspondence with retired senior US military officer, October 2014.
54  Ashraf, 2004; also see Shaukat Qadir, "India's 'Cold Start' Strategy," *The Daily Times*, May 8, 2004.
55  For a discussion of General Musharraf's likely motivations see C. Christine Fair, *India and Pakistan Engagement: Prospects for Breakthrough or*

remain the subject of some debate. Some have argued that he acted on an impulse, others contend that it was made to appease the United States and finally one view holds that he wanted to actually distance himself from the United States and seize the initiative.[56] It is difficult to make a firm assessment of these three competing arguments.

At any event, Musharraf, in an interview with the BBC's Urdu Service in November 2003, reiterated his "four-step" approach to resolving the Kashmir dispute which he had initially proffered at the Agra Summit. They were the commencement of official level talks, India's acknowledgment of the centrality of the Kashmir dispute, the removal of any proposal that was unacceptable to India, Pakistan and the Kashmiris, followed with the adoption of a solution that was acceptable to all three parties.[57]

### THE ONSET OF THE COMPOSITE DIALOGUE

In the wake of the South Asian Association for Regional Cooperation (SAARC) in Islamabad in early January 2004, Musharraf and Vajpayee signed a new declaration.[58] This declaration, for the most part, reiterated past sentiments about the need to end support for terror and also to commence a "composite dialogue" aimed at the resolution of all outstanding disputes including Kashmir.[59] It is pertinent to mention that even prior to the declaration in Islamabad the two sides had already opened a private channel of communication.

*Breakdown*, Special Report 129, January 2005 (Washington, DC: United States Institute of Peace, 2005).

56 For a discussion of these disparate views see Sukumar Muralidharan, "A New Engagement," *Frontline*, 20:11, May 24–June 6, 2003. Available at: www.frontlineonnet.com/fl2011/stories/20030606006800400.htm; for Pakistan's reaction to his call see Jyoti Malhotra, "Jamali Calls Vajpayee to Signal Thaw," *The Indian Express*, April 29, 2003.

57 Musharraf's proposals are discussed in Sajad Padder, *The Composite Dialogue between India and Pakistan: Structure, Process and Agency*, Working Paper No. 65 *Heidelberg Papers in South Asian and Comparative Politics* (Heidelberg: South Asia Institute, Heidelberg University, 2012).

58 Apparently, Brajesh Mishra, Vajpayee's trusted National Security Adviser, had laid the groundwork for rekindling the dialogue process. On this point see Fair, 2005.

59 See the text of the joint statement as printed in *The Hindu*, January 7, 2004.

Pakistan had nominated a veteran bureaucrat and confidante of Musharraf, Tariq Aziz, and India had chosen Satinder Lambah, a diplomat of considerable experience, who had previously served in Pakistan as the country's High Commissioner.[60] Within four months of the Islamabad meeting the BJP-led NDA had lost power in India's national election. The new Congress-led government of Prime Minister Manmohan Singh chose to continue the dialogue that had been initiated under its predecessor. In fact, the new prime minister was passionately committed to the possibility of a rapprochement with Pakistan. In considerable part, he wanted to pursue the dialogue because he was of the opinion that India could not transcend the subcontinent and emerge as a global player if it remained bogged down in a conflict with Pakistan.[61]

Chapter 5 will discuss the evolution of the composite dialogue, its collapse in the wake of yet another Pakistan-based terrorist attack on Bombay (Mumbai) in November 2008, the subsequent attempts at its renewal and its eventual lack of success.

60 Jones, 2007, p. 213.
61 Interview with a retired senior Indian diplomat, New Delhi, October 25, 2010.

# 5

# The composite dialogue and beyond

THE COMPOSITE DIALOGUE AND BEYOND

The precise factors that contributed to the so-called composite dialogue in 2004 remain unclear.[1] However, based on the available evidence it can be argued that it was a combination of domestic Indian initiatives, some reciprocity from Pakistan, and American pressures that led to its onset.[2] It might be recalled that Prime Minister Atal Behari Vajpayee had called for a renewal of the dialogue with Pakistan from Srinagar, the capital of the Indian-controlled portion of the state of Jammu and Kashmir, in April 2003.[3] Pakistan reciprocated his offer and Prime Minister Mir Zafarullah Khan Jamali, in a speech at Quetta on May 18, stated that a dialogue with India was the only way in which outstanding differences would be resolved.[4]

Despite the stated willingness to embark on this dialogue with India, it needs to be reiterated that the structural conditions in Pakistan for a possible rapprochement with India had remained unchanged. The military, with its very expansive view of the country's putative security needs, remained firmly ensconced in

---

1 One account that is widely cited is that of Steve Coll, "The Back Channel," *The New Yorker*, March 2, 2009.

2 On the possible role of US pressure see V.R. Raghavan, "Reality Check on J and K," *The Hindu*, May 17, 2003.

3 Ashok Sharma, "Indian PM Offers Friendship to Pakistan From Behind Bulletproof Glass," *Guardian*, April 19, 2003.

4 Amanullah Kasi, "Dialogue Only Way to Resolve Issues: Jamali," *Dawn*, May 19, 2003.

its political order. Consequently, the fact that the dialogue ultimately collapsed should not be seen as fundamentally surprising. Its seeming promise, in the absence of underlying changes within the Pakistani polity, made it mostly ephemeral at best.

At any event, in the wake of Vajpayee's speech and Jamali's response, a gradual process of normalization ensued with both countries re-appointing high commissioners to each other's capitals, expanding their respective staffs and starting intensive negotiations. These efforts managed to restore road, rail and air links. This process of normalization was helped along with increased exchanges of parliamentarians, businessmen, journalists and academics.[5]

At the outset, India chose to resume a popular bus service and agreed to release 130 Pakistanis who were incarcerated in the country.[6] Almost immediately, in a striking departure from its previous stance, the Minister for External Affairs, Yashwant Sinha, dropped India's long-standing demand that Pakistan end its support for terror as a necessary precondition for talks.[7]

Unfortunately, the issue re-surfaced as General Musharraf sought to embarrass India on the Kashmir question in September at the United Nations General Assembly (UNGA). On the eve of the annual General Assembly session, the Pakistani Permanent Representative to the United Nations, Munir Akram, sent a formal letter complaining that India had evinced little interest in "moving toward a genuine peace process for peace and security in South Asia." Indian analysts believed that this abrupt statement was a precursor to Pakistan's interest in focusing international attention on the Kashmir dispute and away from its dalliance with terror.[8] Not surprisingly, General Musharraf, at a one-day summit on global terror, just prior to the opening of the UNGA session, sought

5  P.R. Chari, Pervaiz Iqbal Cheema and Stephen P. Cohen, *Four Crises and a Peace Process: American Engagement in South Asia* (Washington, DC: Brookings, 2007).

6  Associate Press, "India Reopens Route to Peace with Pakistan: Latest Initiative Will Resume Popular Bus Service Between Countries and Free Pakistani Prisoners," *The Gazette* (Montreal), May 27, 2003; also see Edward Luce, "India Plans Steps to Woo Pakistan," *Financial Times*, May 28, 2003.

7  V. Raghunathan, "India Scraps One Proviso for Talks with Pakistan," *The Straits Times* (Singapore), May 27, 2003.

8  B. Muralidhar Reddy, "Pak. Complaint to U.N. Against India a Surprise," *The Hindu*, August 24, 2003.

to link the Kashmir issue to terrorism, implicitly accusing India of state-sponsored terror.[9] Faced with this Pakistani diplomatic offensive, Prime Minister Atal Behari Vajpayee reiterated India's earlier position on negotiations, namely, that meaningful discussions could only resume when Pakistan had eschewed all support for terror.[10]

Despite this Pakistani posturing at the United Nations and India's forceful response, in late October the Indian Minister for External Affairs, Yashwant Sinha, spelled out a number of measures designed to encourage a resumption of talks. They included a willingness to discuss the restoration of air links, the subsequent resumption of rail services, an increase in bus services between New Delhi and Lahore, and establishing links between the respective coast guards.[11] After some hesitation, no doubt reflecting internal debates within Pakistan's politico-military establishment, it finally chose to respond to the Indian offers toward the end of October. However, Pakistani officials continued to stress the importance of resolving the Kashmir dispute.[12] Though information remains quite scant, it is widely believed that quiet, back-channel talks between the Indian National Security Adviser, Brajesh Mishra, and the Secretary of Pakistan's National Security Council, Tariq Aziz, paved the way for the renewal of negotiations.[13] Both individuals had enjoyed the trust of their respective superiors and thereby were in a position to make meaningful commitments.

Very possibly as a consequence of these private discussions, in November 2003, Pakistan's Foreign Minister Zafarullah Khan Jamali proposed a ceasefire along the LoC in Kashmir and also banned three Islamist militant groups in Pakistan, the Tehreek

9 Mark Turner, "Pakistan President Makes Plea for Kashmir TERROR SUMMIT," *Financial Times*, September 23, 2003.

10 Edward Luce and Mark Turner, "We'll Talk Only When Terror Ends, India's Leader Tells UN," *Financial Times*, September 26, 2003.

11 Rama Lakshmi, "India Pushes New Ties With Pakistan: Delhi Rejects Bilateral Talks on Kashmir," *Washington Post*, October 23, 2003; also see David Rohde, "India Proposes Steps Aimed at Normalizing Ties With Pakistan," *New York Times*, October 22, 2003.

12 Hasan Akhtar, "Pakistan Accepts Most CBMs, Adds New Steps: Sustained Dialogue on Kashmir Stressed," *Dawn*, October 30, 2003.

13 Jyoti Malhotra, "Brajesh, Aziz did Spadework to Bury Past," *The Indian Express*, January 6, 2004; on this subject also see Zahid Hussain, *Frontline Pakistan: The Struggle With Militant Islam* (New York: Columbia University Press, 2007), pp. 113–114.

Pakistan, the Milat-e-Islami and the Khudamul Islam.[14] Almost immediately New Delhi responded positively to this ceasefire offer and it went into effect within a day.[15]

As had happened on many a prior occasion, the SAARC proved to be a propitious occasion for the two sides to hold high-level discussions on its sidelines. To that end, Prime Minister Vajpayee chose to inaugurate the SAARC Information Minster's Conference in New Delhi in early November to prepare the ground for his visit to Islamabad for the annual summit in January 2004.[16] Furthermore, no doubt in an effort to signal a willingness to reduce tensions, India chose to draw down security forces in the portion of Kashmir under its control.[17] Even as India signaled a willingness to resume a dialogue, developments within Pakistan showed that Musharraf was now vulnerable to domestic extremists. In mid-December his motorcade narrowly escaped a bomb blast as it passed over a bridge on his way to Army House after having landed in Islamabad airport.[18]

As the summit approached Musharraf quite abruptly announced that he was willing to set aside Pakistan's hitherto unyielding stance on the UN resolutions dealing with the Kashmir question.[19] A careful reading of his statement, however, showed that he was unwilling to concede the "centrality" of the Kashmir dispute.[20] Whether or not this gesture also stemmed from an awareness of his domestic vulnerability from terrorism remains unclear.

These developments no doubt created propitious conditions for a meeting between Prime Minister Vajpayee and President Musharraf

14  See Syed Moshin Naqvi, "Pakistan Bans Three Islamic Militant Groups,"
    *CNN.* Downloaded on May 26, 2011. Available at: http://articles.cnn.com/
    2003-11-15/world/pakistan.crackdown_1_groups-pakistani-government-
    pakistani-officials?_s=PM:WORLD.
15  Amit Baruah and Sandeep Dikshit, "India, Pak. Ceasefire Comes Into Being,"
    *The Hindu,* November 26, 2003.
16  "SAARC Turns Cover For PM's Pak Visit," *Indian Express,* November 6, 2003.
17  M. Ziauddin, "Delhi Reduces Troop Presence in Kashmir," *Dawn,*
    December 31, 2003.
18  Dawn Report, "Musharraf's Convoy Escapes Bomb Blast," *Dawn,*
    December 15, 2003; also see David Rohde, "Pakistan Bombing Aimed at
    Military Ruler Highlights His Role," *New York Times,* December 24, 2003.
19  John Lancaster, "Pakistan Would Forgo Kashmir Referendum," *Washington
    Post,* December 19, 2003.
20  R. Muralidhar Reddy, "We Have 'Left Aside' U.N. Resolutions on
    Kashmir,: Musharraf," *The Hindu,* December 19, 2003.

at the 12th summit of the SAARC, held in Islamabad between January 2 and 6, 2004. According to an informed observer, the Indian National Security Adviser, Brajesh Mishra, helped prepare the ground for a meeting between the two national leaders.[21] Prior to this meeting, Mishra had also been in contact with the head of the ISI, Lieutenant-General Ehsan ul-Haq. A noted Pakistani analyst has claimed that these discussions had even been kept secret from the Pakistani Foreign Office. Only the Chief of Army Staff, General Hamid and Tariq Aziz had been involved in the involved in the drafting of the joint communiqué that would ensue from this meeting. The Pakistani Foreign Secretary, Riaz Khokar, had been given a copy of the communiqué a mere few hours before its release.[22]

This characterization of the decision-making comports quite well with one of the central arguments of this work, namely, that key choices involving India or the Kashmir dispute have been and remain the preserve of the military establishment. Obviously with Musharraf in power such policy choices were the clear preserve of the military apparatus.

Several other factors apparently also played a role in facilitating this meeting and giving it substance. Under sustained American and British pressure Musharraf had actually taken steps to curb militant infiltration into Indian-controlled Kashmir.[23] Furthermore, earlier agreements on the resumption of bus, air and train services had also helped to contribute to an atmosphere of goodwill. Additionally, developments within Pakistan may have also made Musharraf re-assess and re-calculate his options. Specifically, Musharraf had survived two assassination attempts in December 2003. These events may have convinced him that some of the forces that he had encouraged could now be turning their guns on him and that he needed to rein in their activities.[24]

---

21 C. Christine Fair, *India and Pakistan Engagement: Prospects for Breakthrough or Breakdown? Special Report* 129 (Washington, DC: United States Institute of Peace, 2005).

22 Hussain, 2007, p. 116.

23 On the international pressure on Musharraf see Bushra Asif and Sean Farrell, "India-Pakistan: Breaking the Deadlock," *South Asia Monitor* (Washington, DC: South Asia Program Center for Strategic and International Studies), February 1, 2004.

24 Praful Bidwai, "Towards a Breakthrough," *Frontline*, 21:2, January 17–30, 2004; for evidence that the risks posed to General Musharraf from domestic

Shortly after the summit drew to a close, at a joint statement in Islamabad the two leaders reaffirmed their interest in resuming a dialogue.[25] According to Indian commentators, one of the critical determinants of India's willingness to resume negotiations stemmed from President Musharraf's concession that India's concerns about terror would be within the purview of any discussions.[26] Foreign observers also confirmed that this concession was critical to the resumption of the interrupted dialogue.[27]

### GETTING TO ROUND ONE

Prior to the initial dialogue with Pakistan, no doubt with an eye toward preventing hostile domestic forces from derailing discussions India's Deputy Prime Minister, Lal Krishna Advani, started negotiations with the separatist umbrella organization, the APHC in late January. These talks proved to be somewhat fruitful as both sides agreed to eschew "all forms of violence."[28]

The initial round of the "composite dialogue" was held in Islamabad in February 2004 between two foreign secretaries, Riaz Khokar of Pakistan and Shashank of India.[29] At this meeting, the two sides decided on a basket of eight issues that would be tackled in the course of their dialogue. These included territorial disputes (related to Jammu and Kashmir, the Siachen Glacier and Sir Creek), security questions (terrorism, drug trafficking and conventional as well as nuclear CBMs), commercial/resource related issues

terror probably played a role in his willingness to rein in domestic terrorists see Amy Waldman, "Sense of Mortality Gave Push to India-Pakistan Talks," *New York Times*, January 8, 2004; also see Martin Woollacott, "After Half a Century, a Moment for Optimism: India and Pakistan Have Seized the Initiative From Extremists," *Guardian* (London), January 9, 2004.

25 Amit Baruah and B. Muralidhar Reddy, "India, Pakistan to Start Dialogue in February," *The Hindu*, January 7, 2004.

26 Harish Khare, "Musharraf's Decision Led to Breakthrough," *The Hindu*, January 8, 2004.

27 John Lancaster, "Pakistan and India Agree to Hold Talks; Nuclear Rivals Attempt to End Decades of Strife," *Washington Post*, January 7, 2004.

28 Randeep Ramesh, "Kashmir Talks Yield Promise of Peace," *Guardian* (London), January 23, 2004.

29 Shaukat Piracha, "Indo-Pak Composite Dialogue from May," *The Daily Times* (Lahore), February 19, 2004.

(Wullar Barrage/Tulbul project, trade) and the expansion of people to people contacts.[30]

In May 2004, following the national elections, the BJP-led NDA government was replaced with the Congress-led UPA. Nevertheless, the dialogue continued at the level of the foreign secretaries and they met again in June of the same year.[31] At this meeting the two sides agreed to pre-notify each other about missile tests.[32] The other agreements reached at this meeting were limited and included issues related to the release of fishermen who had strayed into each other's territorial waters, an expansion of consulates and the early release of each other's civilian prisoners. They failed, however, to make any specific progress on the Kashmir question.[33] Additionally, a host of other meetings were held in the summer dealing with a range of functional issues ranging from the sharing of water resources to the curbing of illegal drug traffic.[34] Apart from progress in these areas another minor breakthrough took place in the nuclear realm. The two sides reaffirmed their unilateral commitments not to conduct any further nuclear tests and established a dedicated and secure hotline linking the foreign secretaries of their respective countries.[35] Subsequently, in July at a meeting of the SAARC foreign ministers in Islamabad, they agreed to meet in New Delhi in early September to carry forward the "composite dialogue." Prior to their meeting in September, an effort was made to tackle the long-standing Siachen Glacier dispute. To that end, the defense secretaries of the two countries held discussions. However, beyond agreeing to continue discussions they made little tangible progress.[36]

---

30 Press Trust of India, "India, Pak Agree on Five-Point Agenda," *The Times of India* (New Delhi), February 18, 2004.

31 Amit Baruah, "India, Pakistan Discuss Peace and Security," *The Hindu*, June 28, 2004.

32 Press Trust of India, "India, Pak Agree to Pre-Notification of Missile Tests," *The Times of India*, June 28, 2004.

33 Amy Waldman, "India-Pakistan Talks Make No Specific Gains on Kashmir," *The New York Times*, June 29, 2004.

34 Amit Baruah, "A Season for Talks," *The Hindu*, June 16, 2004.

35 Siddharth Varadarajan, "India, Pak to Ban Nuclear Tests," *The Times of India*, June 20, 2004; also see Randeep Ramesh, "India and Pakistan Cut Risk of War," *Guardian* (London), June 21, 2004

36 Sandeep Dikshit, "India, Pakistan Agree to Continue Talks on Siachen," *The Hindu*, August 7, 2004.

On the eve of the next phase of the "composite dialogue" a resolution passed at the meeting of the All-India Congress Committee offered qualified support for the dialogue. However, it expressed misgivings about Pakistan's unwillingness to eschew the use of terror.[37] Not surprisingly, the allusion to Pakistan's involvement with terror prompted a strong reaction from Islamabad.[38]

### ON TO ROUND TWO

The second round of the dialogue commenced in early September of 2004 between the two foreign ministers, K. Natwar Singh and Khurshid Mehmood Kasuri. From press reports it could be gleaned that the talks made little headway.[39] Both sides focused on their familiar bugbears: India on Pakistan's support for terror in Kashmir and Pakistan on the unresolved Kashmir dispute.[40] Though this round failed to make much headway, Prime Minister Singh met with General Musharraf at the UNGA session in late September. Their discussions ended on an upbeat note even though they did not reach agreement on any concrete issues.[41] Nevertheless, reports from the Pakistani press suggested that the informal discussion proved to be useful in moving the dialogue forward.[42]

Probably with an eye toward promoting a more conducive climate for the upcoming talks in November, New Delhi unilaterally chose to further reduce troops in Indian-controlled Kashmir, arguing that "an improvement in the security situation" in the region

---

37  On the contents of the resolution see B. Muralidhar Reddy, "Rhetoric and Reality," *The Hindu* (Chennai), August 25, 2004.

38  Edward Luce, "Indian 'Propaganda' Irks Islamabad CROSS-BORDER PEACE TALKS," *Financial Times*, August 26, 2004.

39  Edward Luce, "Kashmir Still Divides India and Pakistan Peace Process," *Financial Times*, September 7, 2004.

40  Beth Duff Brown, "India, Pakistan Spar Over Handling Kashmir Dispute," *The Globe and Mail* (Canada), September 6, 2004.

41  Kim Gamel, Associated Press, "India, Pakistan Move Toward 'a New Beginning'; Leaders Tackle Range of Issues in Meeting," *The Globe and Mail* (Canada), September 25, 2004.

42  Hasan Akhtar, "NY Round Broke New Ground: FO," *Dawn*, September 28, 2004.

along with a decline in infiltration from Pakistan justified the troop reductions.[43] To further demonstrate a commitment to the peace process the government of Prime Minister Manmohan Singh also renewed an offer to hold discussions with separatists in Jammu and Kashmir.[44]

These gestures were designed to convey a message to Islamabad about the sincerity of India's intentions. Unfortunately, as the next Foreign Secretary-level talks in late December would soon demonstrate, Islamabad did not construe these as costly signals.[45] From the Pakistani standpoint, no progress had been made on the core issue of the Kashmir dispute.[46]

Despite this continuing impasse on the question of Kashmir, the momentum in the discussions did not come to a close. In late January of 2005, New Delhi announced that a veteran Indian diplomat, Satinder Lambah, who had been India's ambassador to Afghanistan, would start back-channel talks with President Musharraf's security adviser, Tariq Aziz. (India's national security adviser, J.N. Dixit, who had played a critical role in prior discussions with Pakistan, died of a heart attack in early January 2005. M.K. Narayanan, a former director of India's Intelligence Bureau, succeeded him as the national security adviser.)[47]

The most immediate development of any consequence was an agreement forged to start a bus service linking Srinagar, the capital of Indian-controlled Kashmir and Muzzafarabad, the capital of Pakistan-controlled Kashmir respectively in mid-February. This came about in the wake of the Indian Minister of External Affairs,

43 Amy Waldman, "India to Reduce Its Troop Strength in Kashmir," *New York Times*, November 12, 2004; for further background on the decision to reduce troops see Our Special Correspondent, "Troop Reduction Has Created Goodwill, Says Pranab," *The Hindu*, December 9, 2004.

44 Y.P. Rajesh, "Kashmiri Separatists to Consider Indian Offer of Peace Talks," *Washington Post*, November 18, 2004.

45 On the subject of costly signals in international politics see Andrew H. Kydd, *Trust and Mistrust in International Relations* (Princeton: Princeton University Press, 2005).

46 "Pakistan, India Poles Apart on Kashmir," *The Nation* (Pakistan), December 28, 2004; also see M.A. Niazi, "Not so Composite," *The Nation* (Pakistan), December 30, 2004.

47 "Plans to Beef Up Foreign Policy," *Financial Express* (New Delhi), January 28, 2005.

K. Natwar Singh's visit to Islamabad.[48] The agreement to start a bus service was widely hailed as a vital CBM. It was especially significant because much rancor had developed over the past several months on the issue of India's construction of a hydroelectric project, which Pakistan claimed violated the terms of the Indus Waters Treaty of 1960.[49] Indeed the collapse of the bilateral talks had prompted Pakistan to seek World Bank intervention in the matter, a move that was clearly not to India's liking. Furthermore, Pakistani spokesmen had made clear that the failure to find common ground on the project was bound to have an adverse effect on the ongoing dialogue.[50]

Despite this adverse turn, the momentum that had developed did not altogether stall as Musharraf made plans to attend a one-day Indo-Pakistani cricket match in India in April. While in New Delhi, he was also expected to meet with Prime Minister Singh. To that end, once again, the Secretary-General of Pakistan's National Security Council, Tariq Aziz and Satinder Lambah, the convenor of India's National Security Advisory Board, resumed their back-channel diplomacy.[51]

Amidst these preparations for Musharraf's visit to New Delhi a terrorist attack took place on the nascent bus service linking Srinagar with Muzaffarabad.[52] Predictably, both Indian and Pakistani authorities condemned the attack. The timing of the attack, however, did raise a critical question: to what extent did Pakistan still exercise complete control over various militant and terrorist organizations that were operating in Indian-controlled Kashmir? Those inclined to believe that the terrorist attack was deliberately planned and timed to derail the talks were prone to arguing that these entities were now beyond the control of the Pakistani state,

---

48  Manoj Joshi, "Hand of Friendship, But With Riders," *Hindustan Times*, February 16, 2005; also see Somini Sengupta, "Buses to Span Kashmir Line, Signaling Step in Peace Talks," *New York Times*, February 17, 2005.
49  Jawed Naqvi, "Baglihar Dam Talks Collapse: Reservations Not Addressed: Pakistan," *Dawn*, January 7, 2005;
50  B. Muralidhar Reddy, "Baglihar Project: Expert Verdict Binding on India, Pakistan," *The Hindu*, January 11, 2005.
51  Press Trust of India, "Back Channel Diplomacy Intensified Ahead of Musharraf's Visit," April 3, 2005.
52  Ravi Velloor, "Rebels Target Historic Express: Despite Blast on Tuesday, Launch of Bus Service Will Go Ahead Today," *The Straits Times*, April 7, 2005.

that their agenda was at odds with that of Musharraf and that they would have to be isolated in some fashion to enable the progress of bilateral discussions.[53]

The question of Pakistan's continuing dalliance with terror, however, remained in the foreground even as the Musharraf–Singh meeting approached. On April 14, the Indian Minister of Defense, Pranab Mukherjee, in a public speech accused Pakistan of continuing abetment of terror.[54] Despite this somber reminder, the meeting went well. What, beyond a formal meeting acquainting the two national leaders with each other, was accomplished at this meeting? To begin with, the tone of their public statements following the meeting was quite positive.[55] Beyond the rhetorical shifts a small number of substantive developments emerged from the talks. They included a trade agreement, a new rail link between the border states of Rajasthan and Sindh, a commitment to hand over citizens who inadvertently cross the LoC and the release of 156 incarcerated Pakistani fishermen who had strayed into Indian territorial waters. On the central issue of Kashmir, however, there was little or no progress as both parties reiterated their formal claims.[56] Beyond these agreements, Prime Minister Singh also expressed a willingness to review the Baglihar Dam project. This gesture was explicitly designed to reassure his Pakistani counterpart. According to informed sources, in the dam's proposed form, India could potentially cut off water to Pakistan in the event of a war. Such a move, in turn, could empty the canals that Pakistan relied upon to prevent the rapid advance of Indian armored formations.[57]

Despite the attempts at building trust at the Musharraf–Singh meeting, about a month later when the defense secretaries of the

---

53 Randeep Ramesh, "Defying Bombers, 20 Elderly Passengers Embark on the World's Most Perilous Trip: Suicide Attack Fails to Halt Symbolic Journey through Divided Kashmir," *Guardian* (London), April 7, 2005.

54 Our Correspondent, "Islamabad Abetting Terrorism: Delhi: Timeframe on Kashmir Ruled Out," *Dawn*, April 15, 2005.

55 Jawed Naqvi, "India to Consider Valley Troops Cut: Musharraf Satisfied With Talks," *Dawn*, April 18, 2005.

56 Justin Huggler, "Musharraf Agrees Trade Deal With India as Pakistan Win Cricket Series," *Independent*, April 18, 2005.

57 For a thoughtful discussion of the Musharraf visit from an Indian standpoint see "A Question of Trust," *The Hindustan Times* (New Delhi), April 21, 2005.

two countries, Ajai Vikram Singh and Tariq Waseem Ghazi, met in Rawalpindi, they made only limited progress toward resolving the long-standing Siachen Glacier dispute. Reports from both capitals suggested that the talks broke down over differing approaches toward the demilitarization process. India had insisted on a prior, clear demarcation of extant troop deployments.[58] The Pakistani side had wanted an agreement on disengagement, redeployment, demilitarization and monitoring and verification mechanisms.[59] They did, however, agree to continue the ceasefire arrangement that had been in place.

As part of this composite dialogue process, during the week representatives from the two nations also met to discuss the delineation of a maritime boundary along a disputed coastal strip, Sir Creek, off the coast of the Indian state of Gujarat. These talks, too, failed to make any real headway.[60]

The year ended with yet another exogenous shock. This came in the form of an attack on the prestigious Indian Institute of Science in Bangalore that led to the death of a retired scientist and the wounding of several others. Media reports attributed the attack to the LeT, which had threatened attacks on the institution in the past.[61] Given that the LeT had its roots in Pakistan, this attack did not create a particularly propitious atmosphere for the next round of talks.[62]

### HEADING TO THE THIRD ROUND

The preliminary steps toward the third round of the peace process took place on January 17 and 18, 2006 in New Delhi. The two interlocutors were the foreign secretaries of the two states, Riaz Mohammed Khan from Pakistan and Shyam Saran from India. This round made some substantive progress and led up to the

---

58 "No Headway of Siachen," *The Hindustan Times*, May 27, 2005.
59 Qudssia Akhlaque, "Siachen Talks Inconclusive," *Dawn*, May 28, 2005.
60 B. Muraidhar Reddy, "No Progress on Sir Creek," *The Hindu*, May 30, 2005.
61 Ryan Clarke, *Lashkar-I-Taiba: The Fallacy of Subservient Proxies and the Future of Islamist Terrorism in India* (Carlisle Barracks: United States Army War College, 2010).
62 "Attacks Cloud Indo-Pak Talks," *The Hindustan Times*, December 30, 2005.

enforcement of ceasefire agreements along the LoC and the international border.

In the aftermath of the talks, India chose to remove a brigade from Jammu and Kashmir on the grounds that the security situation had improved and that further reductions could be possible if conditions so permitted.[63] The Indian commitment to an amelioration of the relationship with Pakistan was evident from a statement that Prime Minister Manmohan Singh made in late March 2006. He specifically offered Pakistan a treaty of "peace, security and friendship."[64] The Pakistani response to his offer, however, was somewhat predictable. Though the Pakistani Foreign Office welcomed Singh's speech, it nevertheless stressed that the Kashmir question remained Pakistan's central concern.[65]

The next month saw some limited progress toward the forging of a new set of nuclear CBMs.[66] Subsequently, in May the two sides held talks on the issue of the Siachen Glacier. These talks, which were the tenth round of such discussions, proved to be inconclusive. India had expressed a willingness to disengage from the glacier but only after Pakistan had agreed to clear-cut arrangements for surveillance and monitoring provisions in the wake of the troop withdrawal.[67] Despite the absence of progress on the Siachen Glacier issue, the two sides did agree to a joint survey of Sir Creek, the subject of a maritime dispute.[68]

Against this very mixed backdrop an exogenous shock again provided a disturbing reminder of the fragility of the entire peace process. In early July, a series of synchronized bomb attacks ripped through commuter trains and stations across Bombay (Mumbai)

---

63 "Pak Says It Would Welcome Troop Reductions from J-K," *The Hindustan Times*, February 6, 2006.
64 Jo Johnson, "Singh in Peace Call to Pakistan," *The Financial Times*, March 25, 2006; Somini Sengupta, "As Indian Premier Calls for Treaty, Pakistan Says Kashmir is the Key," *New York Times*, March 25, 2006.
65 Qudssia Akhlaque, "Treaty Possible After Kashmir Settlement; FO," *Dawn*, March 28, 2006.
66 Mariana Baabar, "N-Safety With India Still Elusive," *The News*, April 27, 2006.
67 P. Jayaram, "Siachen Glacier: No Progress in Pakistan, India Talks; Rivals to Meet Again After They Fail to Reach Deal on Pulling Out From Mountain Battlefield," *The Straits Times*, May 25, 2006.
68 Jawed Naqvi, "Agreement on Joint Survey of Sir Creek," *Dawn*, May 27, 2006.

killing 160 people and injuring more than 400. Analysts attributed this attack to the LeT.[69] Not surprisingly, the sheer magnitude of this shock had the effect of derailing the peace process as
New Delhi asserted that it had detected that the terrorists who had
orchestrated the attacks could be linked to Pakistan.[70] Indeed, matters soon worsened because one of the principal advocates of the
peace process, Prime Minister Manmohan Singh, accused Pakistan
of complicity in the bombings.[71]

It was not until the annual meeting of the SAARC that any
attempt was made to revive the talks.[72] The progress, if any, however, was limited with both sides reiterating familiar positions.[73]
Nevertheless the process continued and was explicitly reiterated
at the 14th Summit of the Non-Aligned Movement (NAM) held
in Havana in mid-September. Among other matters, the two sides
agreed to create a joint mechanism for combating terror.[74] Despite
the creation of this entity, when a meeting was held in New Delhi
in November, little or no progress ensued. Indian officials admitted
that they were unable to provide Pakistan with definitive evidence
of its complicity in the Bombay (Mumbai) train bombings. Beyond
this issue they also failed to find common ground on the demilitarization of the Siachen Glacier.[75]

Perhaps because of this lack of progress and facing an election at home, General Musharraf in an interview with an Indian
television channel in December reiterated a four-stage process

---

69  Randeep Ramesh, "Rush Hour Bombs Kill at Least 160 in Mumbai,"
    *Guardian*, July 12, 2006.
70  Randeep Ramesh, "Peace Talks Put Off as India Claims Pakistan 'Hand' in
    Mumbai Bombs: Police Say Lashkar-e-Taiba Militants Behind Attacks: Photos
    of Two Muslim Suspects Shown on TV," *Guardian*, July 14, 2006.
71  Somini Sengupta, "India's Prime Minister Scolds Pakistan Over Terrorism,"
    *New York Times*, July 15, 2006; also see Jawed Naqvi, "New Delhi Freezes
    Peace Process," *Dawn*, July 15, 2006.
72  Jo Johnson, "India and Pakistan to Hold First Talks Since Mumbai Blasts," *The
    Financial Times*, August 1, 2006.
73  Saurabh Shukla, "Back to the Table," *India Today*, August 14, 2006.
74  P. Jayaram, "India-Pakistan Peace Talks Back on Track; Leaders Also Pledge
    to Join Efforts in Investigating and Countering Terror," *The Straits Times*,
    September 18, 2006.
75  Somini Sengupta, "Talks by India and Pakistan Make No Gains On Train
    Blasts," *New York Times*, November 16, 2006.

for the resolution of the Kashmir dispute. Among other matters, this package involved the granting of greater autonomy and the demilitarization of the Indian-controlled portion of the state. Simultaneously, he stated that in an eventual settlement, Pakistan would have to cede some of its territorial claims. He also argued that eventually the borders could be made "irrelevant," echoing a sentiment that Prime Minister Singh had previously articulated.[76]

Did this set of proposals indicate that Musharraf, after his initial intransigence, had come to the realization that he needed to improve relations with India? The answer to this question is the subject of debate. Some Indian commentators, deemed to be sympathetic to Pakistani concerns, argue with some force that he was genuinely interested in fashioning a rapprochement with Pakistan.[77] Others, however, were not so sanguine about those prospects.[78]

### TURNING TO THE FOURTH ROUND

The question of whether or not Musharraf was genuinely interested in achieving a breakthrough with India remains debatable. At any rate, given his public statements, he had created a basis for reciprocity from India. Accordingly, the Indian Minister for External Affairs, Pranab Mukherjee, traveled to Pakistan in mid-January 2007 to continue discussions on a range of extant issues. The visit went well but did not lead to any real breakthroughs.[79]

The vulnerability of the peace process to shocks, in this case to a domestic event, was underscored when bombs abruptly exploded on a train, the Samjhauta Express, traveling from New Delhi to Atari (a town near the Indo-Pakistani border) in February, shortly before the scheduled arrival of Khurshid Mehmood Kasuri, the

76 Somini Sengupta, "Pakistani Says Concessions Could Produce Kashmir Pact," *New York Times*, December 6, 2006.

77 A.G. Noorani, "Agenda for Kashmir," *Frontline*, February 25–March 10, 2006, 44–47.

78 Praveen Swami, "An Explosion on the Road to Peace," *The Hindu*, February 27, 2008.

79 Saurabh Shukla, "Back to the Future," *India Today*, January 29, 2007.

Pakistani Minister for Foreign Affairs.[80] The shock of this horrific incident notwithstanding, the two sides nevertheless chose to press ahead with the planned talks, arguing that terror groups were intent on derailing the progress that had been made thus far.[81] It is intriguing to note that despite this untoward event the dialogue was not discontinued. One can only surmise that it was not interrupted because of a fundamental commitment to its continuation on the part of the Indian prime minister. More to the point, since no evidence linked this bombing to Pakistan, it gave the Indian leadership greater leeway to pursue the talks. This determination seemed to pay off as an agreement to reduce nuclear risks was signed during this meeting.[82]

In the wake of this meeting the fourth round of the composite dialogue took place in Islamabad in March. The meeting held between the two foreign secretaries, Shiv Shankar Menon and Riaz Mohammad Khan, involved a wide range of issues including the gradual demilitarization of Indian-controlled Kashmir, the Siachen Glacier dispute, the liberalization of the visa regime and the Kashmir question.[83] Indeed, in the wake of these talks, a spate of reports emerged that the two sides were actually close to reaching an accord of the Kashmir dispute.[84] Even if these accounts were accurate, subsequent events ensured whatever progress had taken place quickly unraveled.

On this occasion, it was another endogenous shock that placed the proceedings into disarray. This time the shock emanated from the exigencies of Pakistan's domestic politics. Specifically, they stemmed from differences between President Musharraf and the

80 Muzeeza Naqvi, Associated Press, "Rail Attacks in India Kills Scores," *Washington Post*, February 19, 2007.
81 Amelia Gentleman, "India and Pakistan Talks Go On In Spite of Deadly Train Explosions," *New York Times*, February 21, 2007.
82 Amy Yee, "India, Pakistan Agree on Nuclear Pact," *Financial Times*, February 22, 2007.
83 Qudssia Aklaque, "Pakistan and India Agree to Discuss Security Doctrines," *Dawn*, March 15, 2007.
84 "Pakistan, India Have Almost Reached 'Accord' on Kashmir, Says Kasuri," *The Hindustan Times*, April 20, 2007; also see "Musharraf Sees Early Kashmir Settlement," *Dawn*, April 26, 2007; and Ranjan Roy, "Kashmir Pact Was Just a Signature Away," *The Times of India*, April 24, 2010.

Chief Justice of the Pakistan Supreme Court, Iftikhar Muhammed Chaudhry.[85] The particulars of their difficulties have been the subject of considerable press commentary and will not be discussed here in any detail. Instead, suffice to state that much political turmoil ensued in the wake of Musharraf's dismissal of Justice Chaudhry. The turmoil within the country placed the ongoing talks and their progress at some risk.[86]

To compound matters, yet another incident further diverted attention from the talks. This came about as a result of a conflagration in the heart of Islamabad. A radical cleric, Abdur Rashid Ghazi, had been operating from the Lal Masjid (Red Mosque) and had encouraged his acolytes to form vigilante squads. These young men had harassed vendors of music and movies and had been responsible for the kidnapping of six Chinese women and a man from an acupuncture clinic, which they asserted was a brothel.[87] Not content with these activities, they had also attacked Western women, including diplomatic personnel, had started knocking on doors on Fridays to ensure that Pakistani residents of the city were going to their mosques and they even searched trash receptacles searching for empty alcohol bottles. Unable to reach a negotiated settlement with the leadership of the mosque and facing diplomatic embarrassment in the wake of the kidnapping of the foreigners, General Musharraf had ordered a siege of the mosque.

These contingencies, no doubt, helped unravel the composite dialogue. However, it is not entirely clear that the process would have yielded substantial results anyway. The central argument of this work is that the Pakistani military establishment, which remained *primus inter pares*, was unlikely to set aside its fundamental unwillingness to reach an accord with India. Such a rapprochement it needs to be understood would greatly diminish their ability to

---

85 For some background discussion see Simon Robinson, "Musharraf on the Brink in Pakistan?" *Time*, July 20, 2007.

86 "India Worried by Turmoil in Pak," *The Hindustan Times*, May 15, 2007; for a former senior Pakistani policy-maker's assessment of the peace talks as well as Musharraf's domestic difficulties see Moeed Yusuf (ed.), *Insurgency and Counterinsurgency in South Asia* (Washington, DC: United States Institute of Peace, 2014).

87 Somini Sengupta and Salman Masood, "Scores Dead in Battle at Pakistani Mosque," *New York Times*, July 11, 2007.

aggrandize substantial economic resources and maintain their privileged position in the political order of the state.

### THE TRAGEDY OF BOMBAY (MUMBAI)

At any rate, in the aftermath of Musharraf's ouster the dialogue was in jeopardy. However, the swarming terrorist attack that took place in Bombay (Mumbai) effectively brought the process to a near-complete halt. Given the significance of this attack it is important to sketch out the key elements thereof. The attack involved ten Pakistani terrorists, who landed in a fishing village on the coast of Bombay on the night of November 26, 2008. They had embarked from the port city of Karachi on a merchant ship. They had subsequently hijacked an Indian fishing vessel to avoid detection by the Indian Coast Guard. One set of them had used the vessel to land at the Sassoon Docks in Bombay (Mumbai). The others had used a fiberglass rowboat and had landed at an area known as Cuffe Parade near a fishing village.[88] Upon landing they had proceeded to fan out to specific, pre-selected targets using global positioning system devices. Daood Gilani, also known as David Coleman Headley, a Pakistani-American, had previously visited India on a number of occasions and had carried out extensive surveillance of these sites.[89]

The terrorists struck a number of key locations including the iconic Taj Hotel near the monument, Gateway of India; the Oberoi Hotel, another prominent tourist destination; the Leopold Café, a gathering place for well-heeled Indians and foreign tourists; the sprawling Chattrapati Shivaji Railway Terminus; an out-of-the-way Jewish cultural center, the Chabad House; and, the well-known Bhikaji Cama Children's Hospital. Within hours of this well-orchestrated strike it became more than apparent that the police and security authorities in the city were hopelessly unprepared for a terrorist assault of this scope and dimension.

---

88  Praveen Swami, "Terrorists Used Hijacked Vessel," *The Hindu*, November 29, 2008.

89  For a detailed account of Headley's role in the events leading up to the terrorist attack see Sebastian Rotella, "The Perfect Terrorist," *Propublica*, November 22, 2011. Available at: www.propublica.org/article/david-headley-homegrown-terrorist/single.

Worse still, it also became evident that the national government had made few, if any, preparations to effectively deal with a major terrorist attack on a major metropolitan center in the country. As a consequence of this abject lack of preparedness, the responses to this extraordinarily brazen attack proved to be inept, ad hoc and clumsy. Indeed it took India's security forces the better part of 72 hours to suppress the terrorists and restore order. Some observers, however, argued that the sheer scope, daring and sophistication of the attack had simply proven too great for local security and police forces to respond effectively.[90]

In fact, press reports soon revealed the extent of the lack of preparedness on the part of the Indian security forces including the commandos, who had been assigned the task of flushing out the terrorists from the Taj Hotel. One marine commando officer even conceded that the terrorists knew the layout of the hotel better than the men under his command.[91]

## IN THE AFTERMATH OF 26/11

As a consequence of the scope of the attacks, the failure to anticipate and accordingly plan for such a contingency, and a rather poor record in ensuring the country's internal security in general, the Minister for Home Affairs, Shivraj Patil, was compelled to resign. A Congress politician from the state of Tamil Nadu, Palaniapannan Chidambaram, known for his organizational efficacy, replaced him.[92]

Shortly thereafter, India demanded that Islamabad hand over 20 fugitives who were believed to enjoy sanctuary in Pakistan. Among them were the leader of the JeM, and Yusuf Muzammil, a member of the LeT.[93] Within days thereof, a former US Department of Defense official stated that US intelligence agencies had evidence linking the plotters of the attacks to both former Pakistan Army

90 James Lamont, "Security was Overwhelmed by Planning," *Financial Times*, December 1, 2008.
91 Joe Leahy, James Lamont and James Blitz, "Raids on Tourist Landmarks were Thoroughly Planned," *Financial Times*, November 29, 2008.
92 Somini Sengupta, Jeremy Kahan, Keith Bradsher, Heather Timmons and Hari Kumar, "A Security Chief Quits as India Struggles to Respond to Attacks," *New York Times*, December 1, 2008.
93 Saeed Shah, *The Globe and Mail*, December 3, 2008.

officers and members of the Pakistani ISI-D.[94] Faced with growing international pressures, in early December Pakistani authorities arrested eight individuals suspected of having been connected to the terrorist attacks.[95] Soon thereafter, Pakistani authorities seized Zaki ur Rahman Lakhvi, the individual who had been accused of masterminding the attacks.[96] Days thereafter the Pakistani government formally banned the Jamaat-ud-Dawa (a new manifestation of the LeT), froze their assets and sealed their offices across the country.[97]

Despite these Pakistani gestures, passions ran high across much of India. Nevertheless, Indian policy-makers ruled out any prospect of military retaliation against Pakistan.[98] What explained the reticence of India's political leadership to respond militarily against Pakistan given the evidence that had emerged linking at least elements of the country's military and intelligence services to the terrorists? The answer to this question is complex. According to a senior Indian national security official at least three considerations stayed the hand of India's policy-makers from undertaking any precipitate actions. First, they believed that swift military action would have bolstered the Pakistani military establishment and undermined the nascent civilian regime of President Asif Ali Zardari. In their judgment, the military would exploit public sentiment and whip up anti-Indian frenzy. Second, they also carefully weighed the likely reactions of the international community. In their view, an attack would have led many to yet again equate the victim with the aggressor and India's moral standing would be diminished. Third, they realized that an attack would address public sentiment within India. However, they also concluded that it would, in the

---

94 Eric Schmitt and Somini Sengupta, "Ex-US Official Cites Pakistani Training for India Attackers," *New York Times*, December 4, 2008.

95 Farhan Bokhari and James Lamont, "Pakistan Arrests Eight in Wake of Mumbai Terrorist Attacks," *Financial Times*, December 9, 2008.

96 Ravi Velloor, "Troops Seize Alleged Mumbai Mastermind; Pakistan Raids HQ of Militant Group in Attempt to Defuse Diplomatic Crisis," *The Straits Times*, December 9, 2008.

97 Our Staff reporters, "Clampdown Launched," *The Nation* (Pakistan), December 11, 2008.

98 Somini Sengupta, Robert F. Worth, Mark McDonald and Eric Schmitt, "India Vows No Retaliation," *New York Times*, December 12, 2008.

end, serve little strategic purpose. Some camps and training facilities would probably be destroyed but the organizational apparatus of the group that had launched the terrorist attacks in the first place would remain mostly intact.[99] Indeed, it seemed to underscore that India was still not in a position to implement the Cold Start doctrine designed to deal with contingencies of this order. Fourth, some in the military establishment also believe that the UPA regime had a basic aversion to use force despite significant provocations.[100]

Faced with the understandable public uproar in the wake of this terrorist attack, there were some revisions of expectations about what could be accomplished, and so the peace process was halted. Simultaneously, the attack induced the government to bring about some organizational and institutional changes. The revised expectations contributed to a distinct shift in tone when dealing with Pakistan. Instead of merely demanding action against the perpetrators of the terrorist attack, Indian authorities now demanded that Pakistan sever its ties with terror altogether.[101] This demand, of course, was reminiscent of those that had been issued in the wake of the Pakistan-based terror attack on the Indian parliament in December 2001. Also, as in the past, India asked Pakistan to hand over a list of 20 terror and criminal suspects, including Masood Azhar, Dawood Ibrahim and Hafiz Mohammed Saeed. Not surprisingly, Pakistan demurred.[102]

In the wake of the crisis, as the new Home Minister, Palaniappan Chidambaram, almost immediately upon assuming office, moved with some dispatch to push for legislation designed to create a new agency specifically charged with the task of both investigating and prosecuting terrorist attacks on Indian soil. Parliament, not surprisingly, passed the legislation with considerable dispatch, creating the National Investigation Agency (NIA).

99 Personal interview with senior Indian national security official, New Delhi, August 1, 2012.
100 Interview with retired senior Indian general, New Delhi, August 2011.
101 Nirupama Subramaniam, "Shut Down LeT Operations, India Tells Pakistan," *The Hindu*, December 9, 2008.
102 Special Correspondent, "Pakistan Won't Hand Over Terror Suspects," *The Nation* (Pakistan) December 3, 2008.

PAKISTAN'S REACTIONS

The precise involvement of the Pakistani military establishment in the terrorist attacks on Bombay (Mumbai) remains the subject of a debate. Certainly, much circumstantial evidence suggests that there was a degree of complicity. The question that cannot be answered definitively is the degree and scope of such involvement in planning and executing the attack.[103] However, based upon the testimonies of a key plotter of the attacks, David Headley Coleman, and also one of the masterminds of the attacks, Abu Hamza, the ISI was involved in its planning and execution to some degree.[104] Faced with pressure from India and international disapprobation, the nascent civilian government in Pakistan chose to act against the LeT, the organization widely believed to be behind the attack.[105] Soon thereafter, Pakistani authorities also detained Maulana Masood Azhar, the leader of the JeM, another anti-Indian terrorist organization.[106] Subsequently, Pakistani authorities also carried out a raid against an LeT camp and arrested Zaki-ur-Rehman, the individual that New Delhi had named as the mastermind behind the attack.[107] In the wake of these gestures and after rebuffing India's demand to hand over 20 suspected criminals and terrorists, Islamabad sought a resumption of the "composite dialogue." Not surprisingly, New Delhi firmly turned down this request, insisting

103  For the most extensive account that suggests a link between Pakistan's security establishment and the terrorist attacks see Rotella, "The Hidden Intelligence Breakdowns Behind the Mumbai Attacks," *Propublica*, May 2, 2011. Available at: www.propublica.org/article/mumbai-case-offers-rare-picture-of-ties-between-pakistans-intelligence-serv; also see Eric Schmitt, Mark Mazzetti and Jane Perlez, "Pakistan's Spies Aided Group Tied to Mumbai Siege," *New York Times*, December 8, 2008.

104  Josh Shahryar, "Trial and Terror: David Headley Coleman and Pakistan's ISI," *Guardian*, May 16, 2011; also see Barney Henderson, "Mumbai 'Handler' Abu Hamza 'Arrested'," *Telegraph*, June 25, 2012.

105  Saeed Shah, "Pakistan Arrests Militant in Mumbai Terror Probe; Leader of Islamic Group Sees Offices Shut, Bank Accounts Froze After Being Accused as a Front for Terrorism," *The Globe and Mail*, December 12, 2008.

106  Jane Perlez, "Pakistan Moves to Curb Group Linked to Attacks," *New York Times*, December 11, 2008.

107  Saeed Shah, "Pakistan Arrests 'Mastermind' of Mumbai Terror Attacks: Militant Names by India Among 12 Seized in Raid: Islamabad Says Local Courts to Try the Detained," *Guardian*, December 9, 2008.

that Pakistan needed to do more to demonstrate its seriousness about ending its support for and involvement with terror.[108]

## ON THE ROAD TO SHARM EL SHEIKH

Despite this initial rebuff, in June of 2009, India slightly shifted its position. At a meeting of the Shanghai Cooperation Organization (SCO), Prime Minister Singh met with President Asif Ali Zardari on the sidelines. However, Singh made it clear to his interlocutor that no progress on India–Pakistan relations was possible in the absence of Pakistan eschewing support for terror. It is widely believed that third-party pressures, especially from the United States, played a vital role in the easing of tensions.[109] The reduction in hostility continued as the two sides agreed that their respective foreign secretaries would meet prior to the NAM summit scheduled for July at Sharm el Sheikh in Egypt. Indian officials, however, were at pains to underscore that this meeting did not represent a resumption of the "composite dialogue." Instead they insisted that the primary focus of the meeting would be on assessing Pakistan's commitment to end its ties to terror.[110] As planned, the two foreign secretaries, Shiv Shanker Menon of India and Salman Bashir of Pakistan, met prior to the onset of the summit. Little information about what transpired at the meeting however was made available in its wake.

Subsequent to their meeting, Prime Minister Singh and his counterpart, Yousaf Raza Gilani, also met at Sharm el Sheikh in mid-July. This meeting did not lead to an immediate resumption of the "composite dialogue" but did provide the basis for its renewal.[111] Even as it did so, the wording of the joint communiqué from the meeting became the subject of controversy, especially in India. In considerable part the controversy stemmed from India's

108 Sandeep Dikshit, "Pause in Composite Dialogue India," *The Hindu*, February 25, 2009.
109 Lydia Polgreen and Somini Sengupta, "Hint of Thaw as Leaders of India and Pakistan Talk," *New York Times*, June 17, 2009.
110 Subhajit Roy and Ajay Kaul, "First Signs of Thaw in India-Pak 26/11 Freeze," *The Indian Express*, June 16, 2009.
111 Lydia Polgreen, "India and Pakistan Agree to Fight Terror Together," *New York Times*, July 17, 2009; also see Amy Kazmin and Farhan Bokhari, "India and Pakistan Vow to Fight Terror," *Financial Times*, July 17, 2009.

willingness to resume the "composite dialogue" without Pakistan making a commensurate commitment to ending its support for terror.[112] Furthermore, Indian critics were also incensed that the joint communiqué had conceded that "Pakistan has some information of threats in Balochistan and other areas."[113]

Whether or not this constituted the betrayal of sorts that the opposition claimed remains an open question and is probably politically fraught. The most likely explanation for the apparent Indian concessions can be traced to Prime Minister Singh's commitment to continue the dialogue in the expectations of producing an eventual breakthrough. Based upon his past behavior it is reasonable to surmise that he allowed these nods to go through in an attempt to change Pakistani beliefs and expectations. Of course, as subsequent events were to demonstrate, his hopes to induce such a change in outlook on the part of his interlocutors failed to adequately grasp the deep-seated intransigence of the Pakistani military establishment toward India and the tenuous position of the legitimately elected civilian leadership. It also failed to take into account the depth of distrust that had accumulated across vast segments of both the Pakistani state and society in terms of their views of India. This subject, the question of deep-seated Pakistani beliefs about Indian truculence with little or no recognition of Pakistan's role in promoting discord, will be dealt with in considerable detail in Chapter 7.

112  Siddharth Varadarajan, "India and Pakistan to 'Delink' Action on Terror From Dialogue," *The Hindu*, July 17, 2009.
113  Siddharth Varadarajan, "Joint Statement Flowed From Meeting of Prime Ministers," *The Hindu*, July 17, 2009; also see Raju Santharam, "Clearly, India Has Succumbed," *The Statesman*, July 18, 2009.

# 6

## An extension of the rivalry

Pakistan's propensity to provoke, needle and otherwise trouble India is not confined to the territorial dispute over Kashmir. Since the US invasion of Afghanistan in 2001 designed to topple the Taliban regime and eviscerate Al Qaeda, it has also sought to limit India's presence in Afghanistan. This quest, of course, has deep roots. It stems from the Pakistani military establishment's stated need for "strategic depth" in the event of another war with India. To that end, Pakistani strategists have argued that they need to have a sympathetic regime in Kabul.[1]

It is interesting to note that even Pakistan's overt acquisition of nuclear weapons, which should deter a significant Indian conventional assault, has not led to the abandonment of this search for "strategic depth."[2] If indeed Pakistan possesses a robust nuclear deterrent then the issue of relying on Afghanistan for "strategic depth" becomes redundant. Nevertheless, this effort has yet to be abandoned and, as this chapter will demonstrate, the Pakistani security apparatus has made a concerted attempt to undermine

---

1 Of course, it is possible to argue that it is entirely reasonable for Pakistan's leadership to seek as much influence it can in a neighboring state and also to limit the political presence of an adversary.
2 For a discussion of the origins of the concept and its evolution see Muhammad Ali Ehsan, "Zarb-e-Azb and the Issue of Strategic Depth," *The Express Tribune*, July 1, 2014.

India's position in Afghanistan. Pakistan's pursuit of this strategy, once again, has relied upon various proxy forces. These non-state actors have sought to harass, threaten and intimidate Indian diplomats, developmental specialists and even ordinary workers in Afghanistan.

The Pakistani argument is that India's goals and activities in Afghanistan are far from benign. Instead, Pakistani spokespersons contend that India seeks to encircle Pakistan with a substantial presence in Afghanistan, thereby creating a two-front problem.[3] The evidence for India's putative efforts to place Pakistan at a strategic disadvantage, however, is quite tenuous. The argument about India's dubious intentions is made mostly on the basis of inference and attribution.

This chapter will provide a brief account of the past history of the Indo-Pakistani commitments to the country after the US toppling of the Taliban regime in 2001, and then delineate how Pakistan has sought to use a range of non-state actors to dislodge India from Afghanistan.[4] It will be demonstrated that India's choices and actions in Afghanistan have been transparent, that they have focused primarily on developmental activities and have not sought to undermine Pakistan's security. Above all, given that it suffered grievously when the Taliban were in power in Afghanistan, India's policy-makers remain acutely concerned that a neo-Taliban regime does not emerge again in the country. To that end, they have sought to bolster elected regimes in the country mostly through the provision of technical and developmental assistance.[5]

Pakistani policy-makers, however, have chosen to construe India's actions as fundamentally inimical to their security interests and have embarked upon a strategy to inflict as much harm as possible on both Indian personnel and assets. Despite Pakistan's predatory behavior in Afghanistan, India has not resorted to a military response. In part, of course, India has been hobbled from acting

---

3 Zahid Malik, "India Encircles Pakistan," *Pakistan Observer*, July 26, 2010.
4 For two overviews see Nicholas Howenstein and Sumit Ganguly, "India-Pakistan Rivalry in Afghanistan," *Journal of International Affairs* 63, no. 1 (Fall/Winter 2009): 127–140; Sumit Ganguly, *India's Role in Afghanistan* (Barcelona: CIDOB, 2012).
5 For a clear statement of Indian concerns see Simon Tisdall, "India and Pakistan's Proxy War Puts Afghanistan at Risk," *Guardian*, May 6, 2010.

with greater force because of three important constraints. The first, obviously, has been the American presence in Afghanistan. Not until it embarked upon a significant drawdown of forces around 2013, was the United States prepared to let India play a substantial role in Afghanistan.[6] Second, owing to its tragic experience of committing ground troops in Sri Lanka in the late 1980s, Indian policy-makers have been reluctant to introduce significant numbers of security forces into the country. Third, in a related vein, the presence of substantial Indian security forces could actually provoke genuine Pakistani security concerns and thereby lead to even more provocative actions and precipitate behavior. Consequently, Indian policy-makers have been content to provide limited amounts of security assistance and have confined their efforts to the training of Afghan security personnel.[7]

Pakistan's concerted efforts to undermine the Indian presence in Afghanistan cannot be interpreted as a defensive strategy or as a fearful response to what it believes to be threatening Indian actions. Indeed despite evidence of Pakistani complicity in attacks on Indian personnel and installations within Afghanistan, India did not end its "composite dialogue" with Pakistan. On the contrary, its strategy is basically offensive and is rooted in the Pakistani state's expansionist view of its own security needs. Ironically, the Pakistani security establishment, however, has seen its actions as basically defensive.[8] Nevertheless, a dispassionate analysis suggests that it is indeed part of the same strategy that has led Pakistan's security apparatus to challenge India, despite the absence of any extant threat.

As the United States and the International Security Assistance Force (ISAF) steadily depart from Afghanistan, in the absence of swift Indian initiatives to guarantee its interests in Afghanistan, the Pakistani security establishment will inevitably seek to keep India at bay. India's policy-makers, concerned at this prospect, started to

---

6 Press Trust of India, "US Looking at India to Play a Key Role in Afghan Stability," *The Economic Times*, April 15, 2013.

7 Sandeep Dikshit, "India to Train Afghan Security Forces," *The Hindu*, October 5, 2011.

8 For a careful and dispassionate assessment see Larry Hanauer and Peter Chalk, *India's and Pakistan's Strategies in Afghanistan: Implications for the US and the Region* (Santa Monica: Rand Corporation, 2012).

undertake modest efforts to protect its interests in the country. To that end, beyond its earlier provision of training Afghan security forces, in 2014 it also agreed to pay for some shipments of weaponry from Russia to Afghanistan.[9]

## THE BACKGROUND TO INDO-PAKISTANI COMPETITION

To understand Pakistan's efforts to limit India's presence and influence in Afghanistan, it is necessary to at least briefly recount the key elements of India's recent relations with Afghanistan. Obviously, this chapter does not purport to present or recount the details of the India–Pakistan–Afghanistan relationship since the end of the last decade of the twentieth century to the present day. Instead certain salient developments and turning points will be discussed here.

At the outset it needs to be recalled that India had chosen to maintain a mostly stony silence during much of the Soviet invasion and occupation of Afghanistan. In the immediate aftermath thereof, of course, India was one of the few democratic states in the global order that had publicly accepted the Soviet rationale for the invasion.

The politics of this decision are complex and have been discussed elsewhere. Suffice to state that India's decision to publicly accept the Soviet justification stemmed from a complex set of regional, domestic and idiosyncratic factors. At a regional level, India could ill-afford to distance itself from the Soviet Union when it was well aware that Pakistan would swiftly come to play a critical role in helping dislodge the Soviets from Afghanistan. More to the point, the US decision to arm Pakistan to pursue its goal of inducing a Soviet withdrawal made it untenable for India to place its arms transfer relationship with the Soviets at risk.[10] Furthermore, at a domestic level, Prime Minister Indira Gandhi was on the verge of assuming office as an interim government was demitting office. In this interregnum, the Indian Foreign Secretary, Triloki Nath Kaul,

---

9  Pranab Dhal Samanta, "India to Pay Russia for Arms, Ammo it Sells to Afghanistan," *The Indian Express*, April 18, 2014.

10  S. Nihal Singh, "Why India Goes to Moscow for Arms," *Asian Survey* 24, no. 7 (July 1984): 707–740.

known for his pro-Soviet proclivities, re-drafted the initial, planned statement at the United Nations General Assembly and replaced it with his preferred draft.[11] Despite this public stance, privately India did communicate its displeasure to the Soviets. The Indian unhappiness with the Soviet invasion stemmed primarily from the fact that the Soviet invasion had brought the Cold War to the doorstep of the subcontinent, renewed the US–Pakistan strategic nexus and thereby undermined India's security.[12]

At a regional level, Mrs. Gandhi did attempt to reassure Pakistan. To that end, she sent the then Foreign Secretary, Ram Sathe, and subsequently, a former Indian Minister for External Affairs, Sardar Swaran Singh, to Islamabad with a clear-cut message suggesting that the two countries seek a regional solution to the crisis.[13] Their visit and message had little or no effect on the military dictatorship of General Zia-ul-Haq. Zia had quite astutely concluded that the Carter administration was on its last legs. Not surprisingly, he rebuffed President Carter's offer of US$400 million in economic and military assistance and chose to wait out the results of the November election in the United States. His patience was suitably rewarded as the Reagan administration chose to lavish the sum of US$3.2 billion of economic and military assistance over a span of five years on the country.

The US decision to arm Pakistan, India's strategic dependence on the Soviet Union and its concomitant inability to distance itself from the USSR effectively foreclosed any possibility of reaching a common front with Pakistan on the Afghanistan crisis. Additionally, as a consequence of the Indian diplomatic position on the Soviet presence in Afghanistan, it did not command any sympathy with the Afghan resistance for the greater duration of the conflict. Furthermore, with the renewal of the US–Pakistan strategic nexus and close coordination of policies toward Soviet-occupied Afghanistan, there was little prospect of India having any outreach to the Afghan resistance. Instead, it

11 Private communication with former Indian foreign secretary, New Delhi, August 2013.
12 G.S. Bhargava, *South Asian Security after Afghanistan* (Lexington: D.C. Heath and Company, 1983).
13 J.N. Dixit, *India-Pakistan in War and Peace* (New Delhi: Books Today, 2002).

maintained diplomatic ties with the Soviet-supported strongmen in the country, much to the chagrin of the United States and to Pakistan's discomfort.

It was well after the Soviet withdrawal from Afghanistan that in 1992 India succeeded in forging ties with one of the key rebel commanders, Ahmed Shah Massoud, the leader of the Northern Alliance.[14] Despite this incipient relationship with the Northern Alliance, India wielded little or no influence within Afghanistan, especially after the Taliban seized power in the country in 1996 with the capture of Kabul. Worse still, the Taliban regime proved to be downright hostile toward India and quite close to Pakistan.[15] India's problems with the Taliban regime would come to the fore in the closing days of 1999 and underscore Pakistan's complicity in aiding, abetting and providing sanctuary to anti-Indian terrorist organizations. These issues would all converge in the hijacking of a routine Indian Airlines flight from Kathmandu to New Delhi and its eventual diversion to Kandahar.

### THE KANDAHAR HIJACKING

The basic details of the Kandahar hijacking are well known and discussed at length in the introduction. Consequently, there is little need to recapitulate the particulars once again.

The only question that needs to be answered is whether or not Pakistan had any role in the hijacking. To this there is no clear-cut answer. What is known, however, is that the terrorists did eventually surface within Pakistan, and India's efforts to extradite them to India failed. Furthermore, there is little question that the hijackers who belonged to the Harkat-ul-Mujahideen were Pakistan based. Finally, Maulana Massod Azhar, one of the terrorists who was swapped for the passengers, subsequently went on to play an important role in the attack on the Indian parliament on December 13, 2001. The fact that he continues to be at large within Pakistan

---

14 Seth G. Jones, *In the Graveyard of Empires: America's War in Afghanistan* (New York: W.W. Norton and Company, 2010).
15 Carlotta Gall, *The Wrong Enemy: America in Afghanistan, 2001–2014* (New York: Houghton Mifflin, 2014).

certainly suggests that the Pakistani state sees little reason to bring him to book.[16]

## INDIA AND AFGHANISTAN AFTER 9/11

In the aftermath of the terrorist attacks on the United States on September 11, 2001 the conservative NDA regime, in a marked departure from past Indian policies, offered to assist the United States as it sought to forge a strategy to deal with the Taliban regime in Afghanistan. According to a well-known Indian scholar, the United States, preoccupied with its internal deliberations, paid scant heed to the Indian offer.[17] Subsequently, when the United States did seek India's assistance, apparently public as well as elite opinion had turned against working with the United States to topple the Taliban regime. Two considerations apparently held India back from responding more favorably. At the time the United Nations had not granted its imprimatur for military operations. Furthermore, while it did not have diplomatic relations with Afghanistan, India had not declared war on the country.[18] The Indian inability or unwillingness to respond positively to the US overtures effectively ensured that its role in Afghanistan during the initial years of the presence of the ISAF would become circumscribed. Indeed during this period Pakistan became the lynchpin of the US strategy in Afghanistan.

Pakistan's significance to the United States and other ISAF members overrode any Indian concerns at this time. For example, when the United States and its allies allowed the airlift of Pakistani and Afghan Taliban fighters from Kunduz in early 2002, India protested vigorously on the grounds that they would eventually seek to wend their way to Kashmir. These protests, however, elicited no response.[19]

16  Sanjeev Miglani and Katharine Houreld, "Pakistan Militant Maulana Masood Azhar Resurfaces, Ignites Fears of Attack," *Reuters.com*, February 18, 2014.

17  Kanti Bajpai, "Foreign Policy in 2001: What's Going On?" *Seminar*, Annual Issue, 2001.

18  Josy Joseph, "Post-9/11, US Sought India's Military Help for Afghan Ops," *The Times of India*, September 11, 2011.

19  Press Trust of India, "India Protests Airlift of Pak Fighters From Kunduz, Fears They Will Enter Kashmir," *The Indian Express*, January 24, 2002. Some observers dispute this claim, asserting that the United States had a substantial

Even as the United States and others prodded Pakistan to prosecute their war aims in Afghanistan, the Pakistani military establishment did not wholeheartedly share their concerns. Instead it remained preoccupied with the country's eastern border with India. In May 2002, for example, as the Indo-Pakistani crisis stemming from the attack on the Indian parliament dragged on, Pakistan moved troops away from the Afghan front to the Indo-Pakistani border.[20] Earlier, it had moved troops from the 11th and 12th corps in late December 2001.[21]

Even as India coped with the ongoing crisis it sought to play a role in the reconstruction of Afghanistan. Its role, as it spokesmen outlined, was primarily developmental and would focus on the reconstruction of schools, hospitals, roads and other infrastructure.[22] The appointment of a veteran Indian diplomat, Satinder Lambah, as the Special Envoy to Afghanistan, underscored the seriousness that the Indian foreign policy establishment attached to this enterprise. The United States, out of regard for Pakistani sensibilities, wanted to limit any Indian military presence or involvement in Afghanistan. Nevertheless, Indian policy-makers evinced an early willingness to help train the Afghan armed forces.[23]

### THE EVOLUTION OF THE INDIAN ROLE

The significance that India attached to its presence in Afghanistan despite US and Pakistani attempts to limit its role became evident in 2003 when a trilateral meeting was held in Tehran. The purpose of this meeting was to discuss a trade route that would

---

Airborne and Early Warning and Control Systems (AWACS) aircraft in the vicinity and these would have noticed the activity. Based upon personal correspondence with retired senior US military officer.

20  Luke Harding, "Pakistan Switches Troops from Afghan Duty to Indian Border," *Guardian*, May 30, 2002.

21  Personal interview with retired senior US military officer, Washington, DC, October 2014.

22  Our Special Correspondent, "India Has Major Role in Rebuilding Afghanistan," *The Hindu*, January 8, 2002.

23  Our Special Correspondent, "India Offers to Help Raise Afghan Army," *The Hindu*, February 1, 2002.

link Iran, Afghanistan and India, owing to Pakistan's unwillingness to grant India overland access to Afghanistan. Specifically, the talks focused on how to link the Iranian port of Chabahar with the Melak–Zaranj–Dilaram route. The construction of this highway would enable India to have a road link through Iran and Afghanistan into Central Asia, a long-standing goal of Indian policy-makers designed to facilitate trade.[24]

Beyond the effort to create this important road link, India invested in substantial infrastructural projects in the country. Some key examples are worth citing. It helped build a 220-kilowatt Double Circuit Transmission Line from Pul-e-Khumri to Kabul, a 220/110/20 kilowatt sub-station in Kabul and it has reconstructed the Salma Dam Power Project (designed to generate 42 megawatts of electricity) in Herat province. Also, at a highly symbolic level, India constructed the Afghan parliament building.

India's efforts to rebuild Afghanistan went beyond these high-profile investments. It also provided more mundane forms of assistance. It initiated the School Feeding Program under the aegis of which 1.4 million schoolchildren received high protein biscuits. Additionally, it reconstructed the Indira Gandhi Institute of Child Health in Kabul; donated 440 buses, 200 minibuses and 285 army trucks; built five public sanitation facilities in Kabul; constructed telephone exchanges in 11 provinces linking to Kabul; and expanded the country's national TV network by providing the city with an uplink and downlinks to all provincial capitals. Beyond these developmental activities, India also started 84 lesser projects in the areas of agriculture, rural development, education, health, vocational training and solar energy. Finally, it donated three Airbus aircraft along with spare parts for Ariana Afghan Airlines.[25] The catalogue of these developmental endeavors suggests that, contrary to the attribution of sinister motives to India's involvement in the country, the bulk of its aid was for critical needs of reconstruction and development.[26]

24 Our Diplomatic Correspondent, "India, Iran, Afghanistan Discuss New Transit Routes," *The Hindu*, January 7, 2003.
25 Arif Jamal, *Call for Transnational Jihad: Lashkar-e-Taiba, 1985–2014* (AvantGarde Books, 2014), p. 134.
26 Jamal, 2014, pp. 134–135.

Nevertheless, as India expanded its presence in the country, Pakistani accusations about its potentially inimical role started to mount. A significant Pakistani misgiving focused on the expansion of Indian consulates in the country in Herat, Mazar-e-Sharif, Kandahar and Jalalabad. Pakistani officials not only raised their concerns with the United States, but went on to publicly air their apprehensions, arguing that they were being used for activities inimical to Pakistan's security. Afghan officials, however, dismissed these charges.[27]

Despite these Pakistani protests, India continued to expand its role in the country but kept its activities confined largely to developmental efforts. For example, in mid-2006 it signed three agreements with Afghanistan dealing with rural development, educational exchanges and administrative assistance. It also pledged an additional US$50 million in aid commitments to the country.[28] India persisted in its efforts despite certain dramatic setbacks including the murder of an Indian engineer by the Taliban.[29]

As the decade drew to a close, independent observers, even within the United States, started to concede that India's developmental activities in Afghanistan were indeed beneficial to the reconstruction of the war-ravaged land. Richard Holbrooke, the US Special Representative for Afghanistan and Pakistan, when questioned about India's interests and activities in Afghanistan on a Pakistan television channel, declared that there is "no evidence at all, that Indians are supporting miscreants" in Pakistan across the Afghanistan–Pakistan border.[30] It is important to note, however, that these assessments were not wholly shared across the policy-making establishment. Some within the US military, extremely close to their Pakistani counterparts, tended to take the

---

27 Aunohita Mojumdar, "Indo-Pak. Rivalry in Afghanistan," *The Hindu*, September 11, 2003; also see B. Muralidhar Reddy, "Pakistan Reiterates Charge Against Indian Consulates," *The Hindu*, September 15, 2003.
28 Agencies, "India, Afghanistan to Sign 3 Pacts Today," *The Hindustan Times*, April 10, 2006.
29 Manish Chand, "Why Afghanistan Matters to India," *The Hindustan Times*, April 30, 2006.
30 Chidanand Rajghatta, "US Endorses Indian Role in Afghanistan," *The Times of India*, April 26, 2009; also see IANS, "India's Role in Afghanistan Crucial, Says Burns," *The Hindustan Times*, May 11, 2009.

more dire view of Indian activities. For example, in September 2009, General Stanley McChrystal, the principal US military commander in Afghanistan, while conceding the benefits of Indian involvement in the country, also argued that the Indian role was provoking Pakistani fears.[31]

It is important to note, however, that Indian policy-makers remained chary of widening their security functions in Afghanistan. This reticence persisted despite an apparent suggestion from Nigel Shinwald, Prime Minister Tony Blair's Foreign Policy Adviser, when on a visit to New Delhi in May 2006.[32] Even Afghan efforts to court India in this matter produced a circumscribed response. Though the Indian Minister of Defense, A.K. Antony, expressed a willingness to bolster Afghanistan's security, he categorically ruled out any Indian military involvement in the country.[33]

India's reluctance to broaden its security presence in Afghanistan did little to reassure Pakistan or end the intransigence of the Taliban toward India. In July 2008, a suicide car bomb attack took place on the Indian mission in Kabul leading to the death of the Indian military attaché, the political counselor, two other Indian officials and as many as 41 individuals.[34] Informed Indian analysts, even at the time, speculated that, in all likelihood, Pakistan's Inter-Services Intelligence (ISI) agency had helped orchestrate the attack.[35] Their conjecture did not prove to be idle. In less than a month US intelligence sources, on the basis of electronic intercepts, concluded that the ISI was indeed involved in the planning and execution of the attack.[36] The attack demonstrated that Pakistan's security apparatus was prepared to

31 Lalit K. Jha, "Rising Indian Influence in Afghan Causing Regional Tension," *The Hindustan Times*, September 22, 2009.

32 M.K. Bhadrakumar, "Indian Security Presence in Afghanistan," *The Hindu*, May 5, 2006.

33 Express News Service, "Afghanistan Looks for Training, Logistics Support from India," *The Indian Express*, New Delhi, April 9, 2008.

34 Waheed Wafa and Alan Cowell, "Suicide Blast Kills 41 in Afghan Capital," *New York Times*, July 8, 2008; also see M. Karim Faiez and Laura King, "Suicide Car Bomb Hits Kabul," *Los Angeles Times*, July 8, 2008.

35 Praveen Swami, "Making the Water Boil in Afghanistan," *The Hindu*, July 9, 2008.

36 Mark Mazzetti and Eric Schmitt, "Pakistanis Aided Attack in Kabul, U.S. Officials Say," *New York Times*, August 1, 2008.

resort to the use of proxy forces to undermine the Indian foothold in Afghanistan. The irony, however, was that despite the pre-
carious security situation that Indian personnel both diplomatic
and otherwise found themselves in, security at Indian installations in the country was limited. Members of the Indo-Tibetan
Border Police armed with rifles constituted the basic elements of
security.[37]

Despite the cost that the attack had imposed, Indian authorities
did not waver in their commitment to the country. Barely a week
later the Indian Foreign Secretary, Shiv Shankar Menon, on a visit
to Kabul reiterated that India's willingness to assist the regime of
President Hamid Karzai remained steadfast. It is pertinent to mention that a day before his visit and speech in Kabul, that the Indian
National Security Adviser, M.K. Narayanan, had blamed Islamabad
for the attack.[38] The attack obviously contributed to a hardening of
the Indian public stance toward Pakistan's behavior in Afghanistan.
Nevertheless, it must be underscored that India chose not to end the
"composite dialogue" with Pakistan. Its unwillingness to terminate the dialogue, despite growing domestic pressures, demonstrated
that it remained keen on reassuring Pakistan of its lack of hostile
intent. Such reassurance, of course, might have worked to assuage
Pakistan's legitimate concerns if the Indo-Pakistani relationship
were a genuine *security dilemma*.

Pakistan-supported attacks continued to mount even after the
emergence of a civilian regime in Pakistan under President Asif Ali
Zardari in September 2008. The persistence of the attacks demonstrated, beyond any reasonable doubt, that even a democratic-
ally elected civilian regime exercised pitiably little control over the
activities of the military establishment. For all practical purposes,
the security establishment continued to dominate and shape the
scope and direction of Pakistan's security policies. These efforts,
however, had little or no effect on moderating Pakistan's policies
and behavior in Afghanistan, as events would once again demonstrate in little over a year.

37 Indrani Bagchi, "India Not to Undertake Fresh Projects in Afghanistan," *The
   Times of India*, August 4, 2008.
38 Amit Baruah, "Will Continue Reconstruction of Afghanistan," *The Hindustan
   Times*, July 13, 2008.

MORE ADVERSE DEVELOPMENTS

Yet another attack took place on the Indian Embassy in Kabul in October 2009, killing 17 individuals.[39] On this occasion the Taliban claimed responsibility for the attack. In a reflection of India's growing frustration with the international community and particularly the United States, Foreign Secretary Nirupama Rao explicitly called on the global community to exert:

effective pressure on Pakistan to implement its stated commitment to deal with terrorist groups within its territory, including members of the Al-Qaeda, Taliban's Quetta Shura, Hizb-e-Islami, Lashkar-e-Taiba and other like-minded terrorist groups.[40]

Furthermore, on this occasion, the Afghan government darkly hinted that "The interior ministry believes this attack was carried out in coordination and consultation with an active intelligence service in the region."[41] Though Pakistan was not explicitly named, it is more than apparent that the statement involved a veiled reference to the country. Despite this Indian expression of frustration, the Afghan insinuation of Pakistani involvement and US revelations of Pakistan's complicity in one or more attacks on Indian assets in the country, other attacks continued apace. A guesthouse, in which Indian personnel had been living, was attacked, leading to the death of an engineer and a musician on a cultural tour.[42]

Amidst a deteriorating security milieu for Indian personnel in the country, a very disturbing revelation came to the fore. A US government report laid bare that the Pakistani military had diverted funds intended to support counterterrorism operations in the region to purchase weaponry for use against India.[43] For Indian observers this disclosure did not come as a particular surprise. However, it did

39 Sabrina Tavernise and Abdul Waheed Wafa, "17 Die in Kabul Bomb Attack," *New York Times*, October 8, 2009.
40 Nirupama Rao as quoted in Siddharth Varadarajan, "A Reminder of India's Burden and Stake in Afghanistan," *The Hindu*, October 9, 2009.
41 Haroon Siddique and agencies, "Afghans Accuse Foreign Agents of Involvement in Indian Embassy Attack," *Guardian*, July 7, 2008.
42 Emily Wax, "India's Courtship of Afghanistan Comes at a Steep Price," *Washington Post*, April 3, 2010.
43 David E. Sanger, "Revamping Pakistan Aid Expected in Report," *New York Times*, December 6, 2008.

underscore the fact that Pakistan's commitment to counterterrorism was not only partial but was clearly subordinate to its ongoing
hostility toward India.

Tensions have not eased since 2009. Indeed, as the US and ISAF
forces draw down, there is every reason to believe that the Pakistani
military will seek to ramp up its activities in Afghanistan through the
use of their proxies. Even though the focus of this work is limited to
the period from 1999 to 2009, a brief discussion of Indo-Pakistani
discord in Afghanistan since 2009 is nevertheless in order.

Owing to the UPA regime's commitment to try and improve relations with Pakistan, Prime Minister Manmohan Singh renewed the
bilateral negotiations with Pakistan in 2009. He did this despite
growing domestic disaffection with this policy, especially in the aftermath of the terrorist attacks on Bombay (Mumbai) in November
2008.[44] Developments within Afghanistan, however, caused Indian
officials some anxiety, especially in 2010 when President Hamid
Karzai sought to try and mend fences with Pakistan and more
importantly started to make overtures toward the Taliban with an
eye toward possible reconciliation. The latter moves, in particular,
disturbed Indian policy-makers given the organization's well-known
ties with Pakistan's ISI.[45]

These fears, however, proved to be somewhat unfounded as relations between Kabul and Islamabad foundered later in the year.
Kabul went on to accuse Pakistan of being involved in a series of
high-profile attacks in the country. Perhaps reflecting Afghanistan's
concerns about Pakistan's attempts to sow discord within the country especially after the assassination of Burhanuddin Rabbani, a
former mujihideen and head of the Afghan High Peace Council, in
late September of 2011, Kabul signed a security partnership with
New Delhi. Under its aegis, they agreed to boost cooperation in
counterterrorism operations and the training of security forces.[46]

Despite this agreement, India's willingness to step up its military
cooperation with Afghanistan remained tepid. India's policy-makers

---

44 Eric Randolph, "India's Afghanistan Dilemma," *Guardian*, January 8, 2010.
45 Rajiv Chandrasekaran, "Neighboring Countries Wary of Thaw in
   Afghan-Pakistan Relations," *Washington Post*, July 25, 2010.
46 Rama Lakshmi, "India and Afghanistan Sign Security and Trade Pact,"
   *Washington Post*, October 4, 2011.

remained hesitant to adopt a more forthright position on weapons sales to Afghanistan largely because of fears that Pakistan would then step up its attacks on Indian assets within the country. Indeed, India's very reticence to adopt a bolder stance on the matter of arms transfers underscored that far from seeking to encircle Pakistan it remained, at best, a hesitant security partner for Afghanistan despite having compelling security concerns in the country.[47]

The emergence of a BJP regime in New Delhi following the national elections of 2014 may lead to a change in India's stance toward its security concerns in Afghanistan. In this context, it needs to be recalled that under a previous BJP coalition regime an Indian Airlines commercial aircraft was hijacked to Kandahar and led to the release of three Pakistan-based terrorists. With continuing attacks on Indian consulates in Afghanistan, the willingness of this more assertive, if not jingoistic, regime to stoically bear costs may be at question.[48] In this context, it is important to note that both President Karzai and the Afghan National Security Adviser, Rangin Dadar Spanta, were present at the swearing-in ceremony for Prime Minister Modi.[49] In September 2014, the two presidential candidates, Ashraf Ghani and Abdullah Abdullah, after much wrangling and substantial American pressure, reached a power-sharing accord.[50] Almost immediately, the Modi regime in New Delhi welcomed this agreement and expressed its interest in working with the new political dispensation.[51]

---

47  For a thoughtful critique of the Indian position, see Shashank Joshi, "India's Afghan Muddle," *The Hindu*, December 18, 2013.
48  AP, "Indian Consulate Attacked in Afghanistan," *Guardian*, May 23, 2014.
49  Aparna Pande, "Pakistan's Nightmare," *The Friday Times*, July 4, 2014.
50  Rod Nordland, "Afghan Presidential Rivals Finally Agree on Power-Sharing Deal," *New York Times*, September 20, 2014.
51  IANS, "Modi Welcomes Agreement between Afghanistan's Ghani, Abdullah," *Business Standard*, September 21, 2014.

# 7

# Policy implications

What are the policy implications that follow from this analysis? Obviously, various peaceful means to arrive at an accommodation have all failed to bring about any resolution of the dispute. As argued at the outset, the initial, multilateral phase, quickly became embroiled in the politics of the Cold War. Apart from arranging a ceasefire and calling for a plebiscite that was never implemented thanks to the intransigence of both parties, it accomplished little or nothing.

Indeed by the early 1960s they had ended in an impasse. Subsequently, the bilateral negotiations in 1962–3 that took place, under considerable Anglo-American pressure, also failed to produce a breakthrough. Subsequently, following Pakistan's decisive defeat in the 1971 war, even the Shimla Accord reached in 1972 failed to result in a final settlement of the Kashmir dispute and to produce a normalized relationship. Even today, Indian and Pakistani interlocutors have markedly different interpretations of the significance of the agreement.[1] Finally, the composite dialogue of 2003–8 did not result in even the beginnings of a settlement, despite having yielded some possible guidelines for the resolution of the dispute. Though a variety of tactics and approaches have been used, none of

---

1 P.R. Chari and Pervaiz Iqbal Cheema, *The Simla Agreement 1972: Its Wasted Promise* (New Delhi: Manohar, 2001).

them have brought the two parties much closer to the resolution of this intractable conflict.

Given this rather pessimistic set of conclusions what general propositions and specific policy recommendations, if any, flow from the analysis? It is evident that India does not seek to pursue a policy of territorial aggrandizement as far as Pakistan is concerned. Indeed, apart from its pre-emptive action on the Siachen Glacier, it has chosen not to expand its reach in the state of Jammu and Kashmir. Instead, it has behaved as a status quo power. Pakistan, on the other hand, has not been content to let the territorial arrangements in the state rest despite its multiple failures to alter the established order. For all practical purposes, as this analysis has sought to demonstrate, the Pakistani state, however, is not a unitary actor. The security establishment within the state continues to define, shape and implement what it deems to be the country's national security interests. To that end, altering the status quo in Kashmir, and later establishing a firm foothold in Afghanistan, have been its twin objectives. As argued earlier, thanks to the indigenous uprising that took place in 1989 in Kashmir, Pakistan sought to revive its claim to the state through the use of a range of non-state actors. Its ability to influence the course of events in Afghanistan, in turn, increased dramatically following the country's internal turmoil in the late 1970s and subsequent Soviet invasion.[2]

On the Kashmir issue, Pakistan's strategy remains twofold. At a public level its policy-makers steadfastly deny supporting a host of irregular forces operating in Kashmir. Instead they assert that they are primarily interested in protecting the rights of the Muslim population of Kashmir while continuing to underscore their formal, legal claim to the entire state. The second part of the strategy, when faced with substantial evidence of the source of the attacks in Kashmir and elsewhere, is to insist that the Pakistani state has no control over the relevant actors. Indeed even when the orchestrated attacks took place on Bombay (Mumbai) in November 2008, Prime Minister Asif Ali Zardari, who happened to be in India on a state visit, claimed that the terrorists attacking the city were "stateless

2 For details see Mohammed Yousaf and Mark Adkin, *The Bear Trap: Afghanistan's Untold Story* (Havetown: Casemate, 2001).

actors." More to the point, he categorically denied that they had enjoyed any support from the Pakistani state.[3]

Our analysis suggests that the Pakistani state, regardless of what regime assumes office, whether democratic or authoritarian, has not abandoned its fundamental goal of wresting Kashmir from India. This intransigence suggests that Pakistan is far from being a security-seeking actor. Attempting to dislodge Kashmir from India actually undermines its own security as it provokes a much more powerful neighbor. Instead, its behavior is distinctly predatory. Despite this behavior, it has come no closer to meeting its fundamental goal. Instead it has, on every occasion, simply rationalized its own behavior and has sought to find other opportunities to needle India.[4]

Based on the evidence that has been adduced it is reasonable to conclude that the Indo-Pakistani relationship cannot be construed as a *security dilemma*. Despite various Indian efforts at conciliation, short of substantial territorial concessions in Kashmir, no Pakistani regime has abandoned its long-standing irredentist claim to the state. Consequently, Indian behavior cannot be seen as the basis for Pakistan's persistent attempts to alter the territorial status quo.

Under the circumstances, the Indian state, unless it is prepared to concede Pakistan's demands in Kashmir, has little or no option to maintain a certain level of defense preparedness along the LoC as well as the Indo-Pakistani border. Protracted attempts at pursuing a dialogue with Pakistan in an attempt to reassure it is unlikely to yield any substantial results. A strategy of reassurance would have worked if this relationship had been a genuine *security dilemma*. The evidence that has been presented in this analysis clearly suggests otherwise. Instead, India is confronted with a revisionist state which will be unresponsive to gestures that seek to allay its fears.

---

3 IANS, "Zardari Blames 'Stateless Actors' for Mumbai Attacks," *The Indian Express*, December 3, 2008.
4 This propensity is discussed in T.V. Paul, *The Warrior State: Pakistan in the Contemporary World* (New York: Oxford University Press, 2014).

Instead, the best strategy for India in the foreseeable future may well be to adopt a policy of deterrence by denial. Obviously, this failed quite abjectly in Bombay (Mumbai) in November 2008. Despite general warnings of an impending terrorist attack, Indian authorities had lacked more specific information and most importantly had failed to plan for a contingency to deal with an attack of the scope that eventually occurred.

A strategy of denial will entail a threefold effort. First, India will have to maintain adequate forces in Kashmir to effectively thwart a Pakistani attack. Such forces need not be so substantial as to appear threatening to Pakistan. To that end, India may not wish to station extensive capabilities near the LoC that could be used for offensive operations. Furthermore, it will also need to maintain sufficient vigilance along the border and not slacken its intelligence collection efforts. As noted earlier, the Kargil imbroglio could take place in considerable measure thanks to the flawed collection, collation and assessment of intelligence.

Second, it will also have to sustain its counterinsurgency efforts within Kashmir to ensure that any infiltration across the LoC is suitably contained. However, an exclusive emphasis on counterinsurgency will not suffice. Many commentators, Indian and foreign, have repeatedly argued that in the absence of some imaginative political initiatives to address a range of underlying grievances, a counterinsurgency strategy on its own will not sustain the continuing impasse.[5] Bluntly stated, New Delhi has to stop viewing the Kashmir issue as a mere matter of law and order and come to terms with the myriad shortcomings of its policies toward the state. Above all it cannot elide over the substantial human rights abuses that had taken place in the conduct of its counterinsurgency operations especially in its initial phases.[6] Also, in the end India may well have to countenance the possibility of granting greater autonomy to the state in an attempt to assuage long-term resentments. This concession, in all likelihood, will not satisfy Pakistan.

5 Sumit Ganguly, "The 'Flag March' Won't Fix Kashmir," *The Wall Street Journal*, July 10, 2010.
6 Asia Watch and Physicians for Human Rights, *The Human Rights Crisis in Kashmir: A Pattern of Impunity* (New York: Human Rights Watch, 1993).

However, it could bring a measure of political quiescence in the Indian-controlled portion of the state and thereby reduce Pakistan's capacity for fomenting discord.

Third, as a political component of this strategy India also needs to forthrightly address a growing problem, which plagues significant parts of the country. A segment of Indian Muslim youth are now increasingly responding to the siren call of global jihad. Until recently, they had evinced little interest in answering that call. However, it is reasonable to surmise that events such as the pogrom in Gujarat in 2002 may have contributed to their radicalization.[7] Beyond the impact of such high-profile developments there are some structural social factors that may have contributed to their political radicalization.

In considerable measure they have so responded because of a perception of growing social, economic and political marginalization. Indeed much statistical evidence suggests that their sentiments are hardly chimerical. As the government's own analysis has demonstrated, Muslims, as a whole, have failed to make significant progress over the last several decades.[8] When important portions of the country's largest religious minority confronts institutional and social barriers to their advancement, it is not entirely surprising that some within it have chosen violent means to express their sense of grievance and alienation. Of course, these individuals and groups can become easy fodder for Pakistan's efforts to sow discord within India.[9]

AVOIDING PROVOCATIVE STRATEGIES

Even as the Indian state seeks to implement a strategy of deterrence through denial it will also need to rein in certain defense programs that can prove to be quite destabilizing and can provoke legitimate

7 For a discussion of Muslim youth radicalization as a consequence of religious fissures in India see Praveen Swami, "The Making of an Indian Terrorist," *The Hindu*, July 10, 2012.
8 Prime Minister's High Level Committee, *Social, Economic and Educational Status of the Muslim Community in India* (New Delhi: Department of Minority Affairs, 2006).
9 Praveen Swami, "Second Sunrise of Indian Jihad," *The Hindu*, April 1, 2014.

Pakistani concerns. One of these, of course, is India's continuing investment in ballistic missile defenses (BMD). The origins of the BMD program are fairly easy to trace. In considerable part, it stems from India's inability to find a suitable conventional military response to Pakistan's use of and reliance upon irregular, jihadi forces. The problem can be stated as follows.

Using their nuclear arsenal as a shield, Pakistani decision-makers have resorted to the use of jihadi forces to attack India in Kashmir and elsewhere with virtual impunity. As Indian policy-makers have considered (and threatened) conventional retaliation against terror attacks, they have raised the prospect of swift escalation to the nuclear level. Unwilling to call Pakistan's bluff, Indian policy-makers have been forced to stand down. To escape this particular strategic dilemma they have started to invest in BMD capabilities. With a robust BMD system in place they hope that they can actually cope with a Pakistani nuclear attack, maintain sufficient forces in reserve and then attack Pakistan with considerable force. Obviously, this strategy assumes the existence of a very substantial BMD force and one that can render a Pakistani first use ragged at best.

This is a seriously flawed strategy on both technological and political grounds. Technologically, it makes the most heroic demands on India's defense industrial base. India's defense science establishment has made a series of sweeping claims about the efficacy of the BMD forces under development. These assertions, however, need to be viewed with more than a modicum of skepticism. The vast majority of the tests that have been conducted have taken place under highly favorable conditions and ones that may be exceedingly difficult to replicate in battlefield situations.[10]

These technological hurdles, for the sake of argument, may be overcome in due course. However, even if the hurdles are surmounted there are sound politico-strategic reasons for not deploying BMD. Many of these arguments were made in the US–Soviet context during the Cold War.[11] Despite differences in capabilities,

10 Pravin Sawhney, "India's Ballistic Missile Defense Capability is Grossly Exaggerated," *Daily News and Analysis*, April 4, 2011.
11 Charles L. Glaser, "Why Even Good Defenses May be Bad," *International Security* 9, no. 2 (Fall 1984): 92–123.

geographic location and terrain, the fundamental underlying logic nevertheless applies and remains compelling in the Indo-Pakistani setting.

The Indian security establishment may well view the deployment of BMD in defensive terms. However, from the standpoint of Pakistan's security apparatus they can quickly be construed as efforts on India's part to seek both a first-strike capability as well as pursue a strategy of escalation dominance. Specifically, Pakistani interlocutors are wont to argue that India is investing in these capabilities to enable it to match Pakistan at every possible level of conflict. Worse still, they argue that with an effective BMD system in place it can resort to a splendid first strike, destroy much of Pakistan's existing nuclear arsenal and then fall back on its BMD capabilities to deal with a ragged Pakistani retaliation.[12] These views, though seemingly chimerical, cannot be dismissed out of hand. Indeed, there is growing evidence that Pakistan is dispersing, concealing and expanding its nuclear forces especially into the tactical realm to counter what it perceives to be growing Indian capabilities.[13] The principal danger that stems from these developments involves a likely devolution of launch authority to local commanders and the possible loss of control over these weapons during a moment of crisis. Additionally, these weapons may prove to be vulnerable to terrorist interception as they are transported to launch sites. Given Pakistan's political volatility, such a prospect cannot be dismissed as being fanciful.[14]

The most beneficial course for India would be to pursue a regional arms control regime with Pakistan. This pathway, however, is not bereft of difficulties. Polemical claims aside, India's nuclear forces were not developed solely to cope with the threat from Pakistan. Instead it embarked upon the nuclear odyssey largely to cope with the threat from the PRC.[15] Unfortunately for

12 Maleeha Lodhi, "Pakistan's Nuclear Compulsions," *The News*, November 6, 2012.
13 Reuters, "Pakistan Builds Low Yield Nuclear Capability," *Dawn*, May 15, 2011.
14 Julian Borger, "Pakistan's Nuclear Weapons at Risk of Theft by Terrorists, US Study Warns," *Guardian*, April 12, 2010.
15 Andrew Kennedy, "India's Nuclear Odyssey: Implicit Umbrellas, Diplomatic Disappointments and the Bomb," *International Security* 36, no. 2 (Fall 2011): 120–153.

India, the PRC categorically refuses to accept the legitimacy of its nuclear weapons program. It was harshly critical of India following its nuclear tests in May 1998, it was staunchly opposed to the US–India civilian nuclear agreement and reluctantly (after US prodding) acceded to granting India relief from the restrictions of the Nuclear Suppliers Group (NSG). Resultantly, India cannot meaningfully propose a trilateral arms control regime. This obvious obstacle notwithstanding New Delhi can nevertheless place nuclear issues on its negotiating agenda with Pakistan with the hope of eliciting some form of reciprocity. Obviously, given the structural attributes of the Indo-Pakistani relationship such an effort is unlikely to address the underlying features of mutual discord. However, it can help contribute toward improving the prospects of crisis stability in the region.

## CONFLICT TERMINATION?

How then might the Indo-Pakistani conflict conclude? At least two possible pathways can be delineated. The first is based on straightforward Realist premises. Over time, the material gap between India and Pakistan is likely to become so great that regardless of what strategy the Pakistani security establishment relies upon, India will be in a position to cope with these provocations. In effect, the rivalry will simply cease to matter. Pakistan will remain an irritant, but the gap between the capabilities both economic and military will become so great that Pakistan's periodic depredations will cease to be of any significance.[16] The other possible route to the termination of this conflict could come about as a consequence of a substantial exogenous or endogenous shock that undermines the privileged position of the Pakistani security establishment.[17]

There is actually a limited precedent for both prospects. In the aftermath of the disastrous Indo-Pakistani conflict of 1971, which culminated in the break-up of Pakistan, a period of quiescence in

16 This argument is developed in Sumit Ganguly, "Will Kashmir Stop India's Rise?" *Foreign Affairs* 85, no. 4 (July/August 2006): 45–57
17 For a discussion see Karen Rasler, William R. Thompson and Sumit Ganguly, *How Rivalries End* (Philadelphia: University of Pennsylvania Press, 2013).

Indo-Pakistani relations ensued and lasted until the Soviet invasion of Afghanistan in December 1979. At one level, thanks to its
squalid role in suppressing the uprising in East Pakistan, the security establishment had been discredited.[18] Its return to the barracks
made the emergence of a civilian regime possible and also led to
the initiation of a peace process with India. For a variety of reasons
the peace process foundered but nevertheless active conflict with
India remained in abeyance. Simultaneously, during this period
the military asymmetry between the two states was so great that it
was exceedingly difficult for Pakistan to undertake military action
against India.

The situation changed in the wake of the Soviet invasion of
Afghanistan and the US decision to arm Pakistan while overlooking the many shortcomings of the military regime of General
Zia-ul-Haq. Once again, with an elected civilian regime out of
the way, the security forces felt emboldened to pique India in the
1980s. Of course, internal discord within India, first in Punjab and
then in Kashmir, provided useful political opportunities that they
could exploit. That said, Pakistani involvement in both insurgencies
expanded their scope, increased their lethality and prolonged their
duration.[19]

It is, of course, entirely possible to envisage a moment that these
two processes may yet again take place in tandem. Should such a
convergence take place a slow process of rapprochement may then
well ensue, bringing one of the most intractable postwar conflicts
to a successful close.

---

18 For one recent account see Gary J. Bass, *The Blood Telegram: Nixon, Kissinger
and a Forgotten Genocide* (New York: Alfred A. Knopf, 2013).
19 For discussions of both see Sumit Ganguly and David P. Fidler (eds.), *India and
Counterinsurgency: Lessons Learned* (London: Routledge, 2009).

# In lieu of an epilogue

## Indo-Pakistani relations under Narendra Modi and Nawaz Sharif

In May 2014, the right-wing BJP won an overwhelming victory in India's general election. Narendra Modi, a former chief minister of the western Indian state of Gujarat, as expected, assumed the office of the prime minister.[1] In one of his most significant (and indeed unprecedented) acts, immediately after his election, he invited all the heads of state of the SAARC to New Delhi for his inauguration. Obviously included in this delegation was his Pakistani counterpart, Prime Minister Nawaz Sharif.[2] This was seen as a critical gesture given Modi's fraught relationship with India's Muslim community and Pakistan because of a pogrom that had taken place in the state of Gujarat in February 2002 when he was the chief minister of the state.[3]

Indeed, a number of commentators held out hope that despite Modi's background and reputation for hawkishness, the invitation to Sharif as well as the leaders of other states of South Asia presaged an interest in improving relations with India's neighbors.[4] These hopes, however, were soon to be dashed.

1 Shashank Bengali, "Conservative Party Wins Big in Indian Election," *Los Angeles Times*, May 16, 2014.
2 Jason Burke, "Pakistan PM to Attend Inauguration of India's New Leader," *Guardian,* May 24, 2014.
3 Ellen Barry, "Before Taking Office in India, Modi Sends an Invitation to Pakistan," *New York Times*, May 21, 2014.
4 Praveen Swami, "In a First, Modi Invites SAARC Leaders for His Swearing-In," *The Hindu*, May 22, 2014.

In the aftermath of his assumption to office a decision was made to resume the bilateral talks that had been initiated with Pakistan during the UPA regime. To that end, the Indian Ministry of External Affairs in July 2014 agreed to resume a dialogue in August in Islamabad.[5] In the past, prior to most India–Pakistan discussions (especially those held in New Delhi) Pakistani delegations had met with various Kashmiri separatists on the eve of the talks. Indian authorities had routinely protested these contacts but, in the end, they had proceeded with the talks as planned. On this occasion, however, the Modi regime, which had explicitly warned against any such meetings, adopted a different stance. When the Pakistani High Commissioner to New Delhi, Abdul Basit, met with Shabir Shah, a well-known Kashmiri separatist, the new government chose to call off the talks.[6]

Pakistani commentators, not surprisingly, criticized the Indian government's decision to call off the talks.[7] Interestingly enough, many of their Indian counterparts shared the view.[8] These criticisms notwithstanding, it is possible to justify the regime's decision to bring a halt to the talks. As discussed in an earlier chapter, it is far from clear that the composite dialogue actually accomplished much. Pakistan's policy-makers, civilian and military alike, were not in a position to make any credible commitments to their Indian counterparts.

The Modi regime's decision to call off the talks was not wholly surprising. Modi's reservations about Pakistan were long known. Furthermore, his principal foreign and security policy aide, the National Security Adviser, Ajit Doval, a former (and highly regarded) head of the Intelligence Bureau (IB), India's domestic intelligence service, is also known for his skepticism regarding Pakistan.

---

5  Suhasini Haidar, "India, Pak Foreign Secys to Meet on Aug 25," *The Hindu*, July 23, 2014.

6  HT Correspondent, "Pak Envoy Meets Kashmiri Separatist, India Calls Off Talks," *The Hindustan Times*, August 18, 2014; also see Matin Haider, "India Calls off Foreign Secretary Talks with Pakistan," *Dawn*, August 18, 2014.

7  Niharika Mandhana, "India Cancels Planned Talks with Pakistan," *Wall Street Journal*, August 18, 2014.

8  Praveen Swami, "Self Goal: Delhi Shuts Off Life Support to Dialogue," *The Indian Express*, August 19, 2014.

A MORE ADVERSE TURN?

In October 2014, cross-border firing erupted both along the international border as well as the LoC in Kashmir. What led to the resumption of hostilities remains murky. One account, by a noted Indian journalist, suggests that a relatively innocuous attempt to remove some natural obstacles along the Indian side of the LoC may have provoked their Pakistani counterparts.[9] Pakistani accounts, while highlighting the cost of the conflict, did not proffer any explanations for the resumption of border violence.[10] Foreign sources stated that both sides blamed each other for the breakdown in the ceasefire.[11]

Regardless of which side initiated the hostilities, they continued throughout much of October. The Modi regime, not surprisingly, adopted a fairly unyielding stance and made clear that Pakistan would pay a price if it continued to engage in cross-border shelling.[12] It is entirely possible as the winter descends in Kashmir that these ceasefire violations, whatever their provenance, will taper off.[13] The harshness of the winter inevitably makes any military operations along the border all but impossible. What remains unclear, however, is if they are likely to resume once again when the frigid conditions end in the spring. In the past, especially prior to the 2003 ceasefire, there had been a steady uptick in infiltration efforts into Kashmir and concomitant exchanges of fire.

What is also uncertain is the Modi regime's likely policy toward Pakistan. It is, of course, tempting to argue that the harsher stance that it has adopted toward Pakistan will simply continue. Yet such an assertion needs to be suitably tempered. As argued at some length in Chapter 2, a BJP-led regime had sought to fashion a rapprochement with Pakistan. Atal Behari Vajpayee, the then prime minister,

9 Praveen Swami, "Bushfire to Bullets: Face-Off Threatens to Spin Out of Control," *The Indian Express*, October 9, 2014.

10 Imran Sadiq, "Three Killed in Cross Border Firing along India-Pakistan Working Boundary," *Dawn*, October 8, 2014.

11 Annie Gowen, "India and Pakistan Trade Blame Over Shelling Across Disputed Kashmir Border," *Washington Post*, October 9, 2014.

12 Jason Burke, "India Warns Pakistan it Will Pay Heavy Price for Shelling in Kashmir," *Guardian*, October 9, 2014.

13 For an alarmist account that argues how the present tensions could escalate dramatically see Bruce Reidel, "India-Pakistan Head for Nuke War," *The*

had not been previously known for his conciliatory approach in dealing with Pakistan. Indeed, in a previous coalition regime in the 1970s, when he had served as the country's Minister for External Affairs, he had sought, albeit unsuccessfully, to improve relations with the PRC.[14] However, he had made no particular overtures toward Pakistan during his term in office. Accordingly, it is possible that Modi, whose unwillingness to make unilateral concessions toward Pakistan is hardly at question, could also adopt a markedly different approach in dealing with India's long-standing adversary later in his term. That said, given Modi's own ideological predilections, the unwillingness of even the Manmohan Singh regime to undertake any territorial concessions in Kashmir, and his own political base, it appears extremely unlikely that he will return to a strategy of making any unilateral concessions.

Furthermore, the past record of unilateral Indian concessions has not necessarily elicited a substantial change in Pakistani military attitudes or behavior. Indeed, whatever position Modi adopts toward Pakistan his ability to forge better ties will nevertheless remain dependent upon the internal structure of the Pakistani state. In the absence of a shift in the outlook of the Pakistani security establishment, it is unlikely that he will be able to reach any accord that has a binding quality. As argued and demonstrated in this analysis, the Pakistani security order's intransigence toward India is deep-rooted. Furthermore, apart from the brief interregnum of the years after the 1971 war until the overthrow of President Zulfikar Ali Bhutto's regime in 1977 in Operation Fair Play, the military has played a disproportionate role in shaping Pakistan's internal politics and ordering its external relations.[15]

In 2014 the political landscape within Pakistan did not offer any indications that the military's *primus inter pares* status within the country's political dispensation was about to undergo any dramatic transformation. If anything, the Nawaz Sharif regime appeared

---

*Daily Beast.* October 19, 2014. Available at: www.thedailybeast.com/articles/2014/10/19/icymi-india-pakistan-head-for-nuke-war.html.

14  K.P. Misra (ed.), *Janata's Foreign Policy* (New Delhi: Vikas Publishing House, 1979).

15  Anthony Hyman, Muhammed Ghayur and Naresh Kaushik, *Pakistan: Zia and After …* (New Delhi: Abhinav Publishers, 1989).

besieged with multiple crises on a variety of fronts and had evinced little or no ability of tackling them forthrightly. At home, he not only faced an endemic economic crisis but substantial political opposition from both a Pakistan-based adversary, the former cricketing star, Imran Khan, as well as a Canada-based cleric, Tahirul Qadri, who accused him of having manipulated the results of the election that brought him into office. Not surprisingly, possible rumors of a possible military coup were frequently in the offing.[16]

The central issue, it is worth reiterating, is that the Pakistani security establishment remains unreconciled to the territorial status quo in South Asia. Unlike other states, which have chosen to withdraw from territories that they once controlled, or have simply abandoned their claims, the security establishment in Pakistan seems incapable of envisaging a security order in South Asia where borders drawn at the end of British colonial rule are now considered to be final.[17] Given its commitment to sustain the claim to Kashmir, the persistent weakness of civilian institutions and the near irrelevance of Pakistan's civil society when it comes to relations with India in general, and the Kashmir dispute in particular, it is hard to see how a fundamentally alternative approach to dealing with New Delhi may emerge in Islamabad. Under the circumstances the only viable policy alternative for the foreseeable future is to eschew the adoption of provocative military doctrines and strategies that are destabilizing, to rein in technologies that can help foster arms racing and adhere to whatever confidence-building regimes that do exist.

16 Najam Sethi, "Operation 'Get Nawaz Sharif'," *The Friday Times*, September 5, 2014.
17 For a discussion on how states can cede territorial claims and reconfigure their national identities see Ian S. Lustick, *Unsettled States, Disputed Lands: Britain and Ireland, France and Algeria, Israel and the West Bank-Gaza* (Ithaca: Cornell University Press, 1995).

# Appendices

## Appendix A: The Karachi Agreement

**Karachi Agreement**
**July 27, 1949**

### I. INTRODUCTION

A. The military representatives of India and Pakistan met together in Karachi from 18 July to 27 July 1949 under the auspices of the Truce Sub-Committee of the United Nations Commission for India and Pakistan.

B. The members of the Indian delegation were: Lieutenant-General S.M. Shrinagesh, Major-General K.S Thimayya, Brigadier S.H.F.J. Manekshaw. As observers: Mr. H.M. Patel, Mr. V. Sahay.

C. The members of the Pakistan delegation were: Major-General W.J. Cawthorn, Major-General Nazir Ahmad, Brigadier M. Sher Khan. As observers: Mr. M. Ayub, Mr. A. A. Khan.

D. The members of the Truce Sub-Committee of the United Nations Commission for India and Pakistan were: Mr. Hernando Samper (Colombia), Chairman; Mr. William L.S. Williams (United States); Lieutenant-General Maurice Delvoie, Military Adviser, Mr. Miguel A. Marin, Legal Adviser.

### II. AGREEMENT

A. Considering:

   1. That the United Nations Commission for India and Pakistan, in its letter dated 2 July, 1949, invited the Governments of

India and Pakistan to send fully authorized military representatives to meet jointly in Karachi under the auspices of the Commission's Truce Sub-Committee to establish a cease-fire line in the State of Jammu and Kashmir, mutually agreed upon by the governments of India and Pakistan;

2. That the United Nations Commission for India and Pakistan in its letter stated that "The meeting will be for military purposes; political issues will not be considered," and that "They will be conducted without prejudice to negotiations concerning the Truce Agreement";

3. That in the same letter the United Nations Commission for India and Pakistan further stated that "The cease-fire line is a complement of the suspension of hostilities, which falls within the provisions of Part I of the Resolution of 13 August, 1948 and can be considered separately from the questions relating to Part II of the same Resolution";

4. That the Governments of India and Pakistan, in their letters dated 7 July, 1949 to the Chairman of the Commission, accepted the Commission's invitation to the military conference in Karachi;

B. The Delegations of India and Pakistan, duly authorized, have reached the following agreement:

1. Under the provision of Part I of the Resolution of 13 August, 1948, and as a complement of the suspension of hostilities in the State of Jammu and Kashmir on 1 January, 1949, a cease-fire line is established.

2. The cease-fire line runs from MANAWAR in the south, north to KERAN and from KERAN east to the glacier area, as follows:

(a) The line from MANAWAR to the south bank of JHELUM River at URUSA (inclusive to India) is the line now defined by the factual positions about which there is agreement between both parties. Where there has hitherto not been agreement, the line shall be as follows:

(i) In the PATRANA area: KOEL (inclusive to Pakistan) north along the KHUWALA KAS Nullah up to Point 2276 (inclusive to India), thence to KIRNI (inclusive to India).

(ii) KHAMBHA, PIR SATWAN, Point 3150 and Point 3606 are inclusive to India, thence the line runs to the factual position at BAGLA GALA, thence to the factual position at Point 3300.

(iii) In the area south of URI the positions of PIR KANTHI and LEDI GALI are inclusive to Pakistan.

(b) From the north bank of the JHELUM River the line runs from a point opposite the village of URUSA (NL 972109), thence north following the BALLASETH DA NAR Nullah (inclusive to Pakistan), up to NL 973140, thence north-east to CHHOTA KAZINAG (Point 10657 inclusive to India), thence to NM 010180, thence to NM 037210, thence to Point 11825 (NM 025354, inclusive to Pakistan), thence to TUTMARI GALI (to be shared by both sides, posts to be established 500 yards on either side of the GALI), thence to the north-west through the first "R" of BURJI NAR to north of GABDORI, thence straight west to just north of point 9870, thence along the black line north of BIJILDHAR to north of BATARASI, thence to just south of SUDPURA, thence due north to the KATHAKAZINAG Nullah, thence along the Nullah to its junction with the GRANGNAR Nullah, thence along the latter Nullah to KAJNWALA PATHRA (inclusive to India), thence across the DANNA ridge (following the factual positions) to RICHMAR GALI (inclusive to India), thence north to THANDA KATHA Nullah, thence north to the KISHANGANGA River. The line then follows the KISHANGANGA River up to a point situated between JARGI and TARBAN, thence (all inclusive to Pakistan) to BANKORAN. thence north-east to KHORI, thence to the hill feature 8930 (in Square 9053), thence straight north to Point 10164 (in Square 9057), thence to Point 10323 (in Square 9161), thence north east straight to GUTHUR, then to BHUTPATHRA, thence to NL 980707, thence following the BUGINA Nullah to the junction with the KISHANGANGA River at Point 4739. Thereafter the line follows the KISHANGANGA River to KERAN and onwards to Point 4996 (NL 975818).

(c) From Point 4996 the line follows (all inclusive to Pakistan) the JAMGAR Nullah eastward to Point 12124, to KATWARE, to Point 6678. then to the north-east to SARIAN (Point 11279), to Point 11837, to Point 13090 to Point 12641, thence east again to Point 11142, thence to DHAKKI, thence to Point: 11415, thence to Point 10301, thence to Point 7507, thence to Point 10685, thence to Point 8388, thence south-east to Point 11812. Thence the line runs (all inclusive to India), to Point 13220, thence across the river to the east to Point 13449 (DUHMAT), thence to Point 14586 (ANZBARI), thence to Point 13554, thence to Milestone 45 on the BURZIL Nullah, thence to the east to ZIANKAL (Point 12909), thence to the south-east to Point 1114, thence to Point 12216, thence to Point 12867, thence to the east to Point 11264, thence to KARO (Point 14985), thence to Point 14014, thence to Point 12089, thence following the track to Point 12879. From there the line runs to Point 13647 (KAROBAL GALI, to be shared by both sides). The cease-fire line runs thence through RETAGAH CHHISH (Point 15316), thence through Point 15889, thence through Point 17392, thence through Point 16458, thence to MARPO LA (to be shared by both sides), thence through Point 17561, thence through Point 17352, thence through Point 18400, thence through Point 16760, thence to (inclusive to India) DALUNANG.

(d) From DALUNANG eastwards the cease-fire line will follow the general line Point 15495, ISHMAN, MANUS, GANGAM, GUNDERMAN, Point 13620, JUNKAR (Point 17628), MARMAK, NATSARA, SHANGRUTH (Point 17531), CHORBAT LA (Point 15700), CHALUNKA (on the SHYOK River), KHOR, thence north to the glaciers. This portion of the cease-fire line shall be demarcated in detail on the basis of the factual position as of 27 July, 1949, by the local commanders assisted by United Nations military observers.

C. The cease-fire line described above shall be drawn on a one inch map (where available) and then be verified mutually on the ground by local commanders on each side with the assistance of the United Nations Military Observers, so as to eliminate any no-man's land. In the event that the local commanders are unable to reach agreement, the matter shall be referred to the

Commission's Military Adviser, whose decision shall be final. After this verification, the Military Adviser will issue to each High Command a map on which will be marked the definitive cease-fire line.

D. No troops shall be stationed or operate in the area of the BURZIL Nullah from south of MINIMARG to the cease-fire line. This area is bounded on the west by the Ridge leading northeast from DEDGAI KAL to Point 13071, to Point 9447, to Point 13466, to Point 13463, and on the east by the Ridge running from Point 12470, to Point 11608, to Point 13004, to Point 13976, to Point 13450. Pakistan may, however, post troops on the western of the above ridges to cover the approaches to KHAMBRI BAI Pass.

E. In any dispositions that may be adopted in consequence of the present agreement troops will remain at least 500 yards from the cease-fire line except where the KISHANGANGA River constitutes the line. Points which have been shown as inclusive to one party may be occupied by that party, but the troops of the other party shall remain at a distance of 500 yards.

F. Both sides shall be free to adjust their defensive positions behind the cease-fire line as determined in paragraphs A through E, inclusive above, subject to no wire or mines being used when new bunkers and defences are constructed. There shall be no increase of forces or strengthening of defences in areas where no major adjustments are involved by the determination of the cease-fire line.

G. The action permitted by paragraph F above shall not be accompanied or accomplished by the introduction of additional military potential by either side into the State of Jammu and Kashmir.

H. Except as modified by Paragraphs II-A to II-G, inclusive, above, the military agreements between the two High Commands relating to the cease-fire of 1 January 1949 shall continue to remain operative.

I. The United Nations Commission for India and Pakistan will station Observers where it deems necessary.

J. The Delegations shall refer this agreement to their respective Governments for ratification. The documents of ratification shall be deposited with the United Nations Commission for India and Pakistan not later than 31 July 1949.

K. A period of 30 days from the date of ratification shall be allowed to each side to vacate the areas at present occupied by them beyond the cease-fire line as now determined. Before the expiration of this 30-day period there shall be no forward movement into areas to be taken over by either side pursuant to this agreement, except by mutual agreement between local commanders.

In faith whereof the undersigned sign this document in three original copies.

*Done in Karachi on 27 July 1949*

For the Government of India:

**(Signed) S.M. Shrinagesh**

For the Government of Pakistan:

**(Signed) J. Cawthorn, Maj. Gen.**

For the United Nations Commission for India and Pakistan:

**(Signed) Hernando Samper**

**(Signed) M. Delvoie**

# Appendix B: The Tashkent Declaration

## Tashkent Declaration
### January 10, 1966

The Prime Minister of India and the President of Pakistan having met at Tashkent and having discussed the existing relations between India and Pakistan, hereby declare their firm resolve to restore normal and peaceful relations between their countries and to promote understanding and friendly relations between their peoples. They consider the attainment of these objectives of vital importance for the welfare of the 600 million people of India and Pakistan.

I. The Prime Minister of India and the President of Pakistan agree that both sides will exert all efforts to create good neighborly relations between India and Pakistan in accordance with the United Nations Charter. They reaffirm their obligation under the Charter not to have recourse to force and to settle their disputes through peaceful means. They considered that the interests of peace in their region and particularly in the Indo-Pakistan Sub-Continent and, indeed, the interests of the peoples of India and Pakistan were not served by the continuance of tension between the two countries. It was against this background that Jammu and Kashmir was discussed, and each of the sides set forth its respective position.

II. The Prime Minister of India and the President of Pakistan have agreed that all armed personnel of the two countries shall be withdrawn not later than 25 February 1966 to the positions they held prior to 5 August 1965, and both sides shall observe the cease-fire terms on the cease-fire line.

III. The Prime Minister of India and the President of Pakistan have agreed that relations between India and Pakistan shall be based on the principle of non-interference in the internal affairs of each other.

IV. The Prime Minister of India and the President of Pakistan have agreed that both sides will discourage any propaganda directed against the other country, and will encourage propaganda which promotes the development of friendly relations between the two countries.

V. The Prime Minister of India and the President of Pakistan have agreed that the High Commissioner of India to Pakistan and the High Commissioner of Pakistan to India will return to their posts and that the normal functioning of diplomatic missions of both countries will be restored. Both Governments shall observe the Vienna Convention of 1961 on Diplomatic Intercourse.

VI. The Prime Minister of India and the President of Pakistan have agreed to consider measures towards the restoration of economic and trade relations, communications, as well as cultural exchanges between India and Pakistan, and to take measures to implement the existing agreements between India and Pakistan.

VII. The Prime Minister of India and the President of Pakistan have agreed that they will give instructions to their respective authorities to carry out the repatriation of the prisoners of war.

VIII. The Prime Minister of India and the President of Pakistan have agreed that the two sides will continue the discussion of questions relating to the problems of refugees and eviction/illegal immigrations. They also agreed that both sides will create conditions which will prevent the exodus of people. They further agree to discuss the return of the property and assets taken over by either side in connection with the conflict.

IX. The Prime Minister of India and the President of Pakistan
have agreed that the two sides will continue meetings both
at highest and at other levels of matters of direct concern to
both countries. Both sides have recognized the need to set
up joint Indian-Pakistani bodies which will report to their
Governments in order to decide what further steps should
be taken.

The Prime Minister of India and the President of Pakistan record
their feelings of deep appreciation and gratitude to the leaders of
the Soviet Union, the Soviet Government and personally to the
Chairman of the Council of Ministers of the USSR for their con-
structive, friendly and noble part in bringing about the present
meeting which has resulted in mutually satisfactory results. They
also express to the Government and friendly people of Uzbekistan
their sincere thankfulness for their overwhelming reception and
generous hospitality.

They invite the Chairman of the Council of Ministers of the
U.S.S.R to witness this Declaration.

**(Signed) Lal Bahadur**

Prime Minister of India

**(Signed) M.A. Khan, F.M.**

President of Pakistan

**Tashkent, 10 January 1966.**

# Appendix C: The Shimla Agreement

**Shimla Agreement**
**July 2, 1972**

1. The Government of India and the Government of Pakistan are resolved that the two countries put an end to the conflict and confrontation that have hitherto marred their relations and work for the promotion of a friendly and harmonious relationship and the establishment of durable peace in the sub-continent, so that both countries may henceforth devote their resources and energies to the pressing task of advancing the welfare of their peoples.

In order to achieve this objective, the Government of India and the Government of Pakistan have agreed as follows:

   I. That the principles and purposes of the Charter of the United Nations shall govern the relations between the two countries;

   II. That the two countries are resolved to settle their differences by peaceful means through bilateral negotiations or by any other peaceful means mutually agreed upon between them. Pending the final settlement of any of the problems between the two countries, neither side shall unilaterally alter the situation and both shall prevent the organization, assistance of encouragement of any acts detrimental to the maintenance of peaceful and harmonious relations;

III. That the pre-requisites for reconciliation, good neighbor-liness and durable peace between them is a commitment by both the countries to peaceful co-existence, respect for each other's territorial integrity and sovereignty and non-interference in each other's internal affairs, on the basis of equality and mutual benefit;

IV. That the basic issues and causes of conflict which have bedeviled the relations between the two countries for the last 25 years shall be resolved by peaceful means;

V. That there shall always respect each other's national unity, territorial integrity, political independence and sovereign equality;

VI. That in accordance with the Charter of the United Nations they will refrain from the threat of use force against the ter-ritorial integrity or political independence of each other;

2. Both Governments will take steps within their power to prevent hostile propaganda directed against each other. Both countries will encourage the dissemination of such information as would promote the development of friendly relations between them.

3. In order progressively to restore and normalize relations between the two countries step by step, it was agreed that:

I. Steps shall be taken to resume communications, postal, telegraphic, sea, land including border posts, and air links including overflights;

II. Appropriate steps shall be taken to promote travel facilities for the nationals of the other country;

III. Trade and cooperation in economic and other agreed fields will be resumed as far as possible;

IV. Exchange in the fields of science and culture will be promoted;

In this connection delegations from the two countries will meet from time to time to work out the necessary details.

4. In order to initiate the process of establishment of durable peace, both the Governments agree that:

I. Indian and Pakistani forces shall be withdrawn to their side of the international border;

II. In Jammu and Kashmir, the line of control resulting from the cease-fire of December 17, 1971 shall be respected by both sides without prejudice to the recognized position of either side. Neither side shall seek to alter it unilaterally, irrespective of mutual differences and legal interpretations. Both sides further undertake to refrain from the threat or the use of force in violation of this Line;

III. The withdrawals shall commence upon entry into force of this Agreement and shall be completed within a period of 30 days thereof;

IV. This Agreement will be subject to ratification by both countries in accordance with their respective constitutional procedures and will come into force with effect from the date on which the Instruments of ratification are exchanged;

5. Both Governments agree that their respective Heads will meet again at a mutually convenient time in the future and that, in the meanwhile, the representatives of the two sides will meet to discuss further the modalities and arrangements for the establishment of durable peace and normalization of relations, including the questions of repatriation of prisoners of war and civilian internees, a final settlement of Jammu and Kashmir and the resumption of diplomatic relations.

(Signed) **Indira Gandhi**

Prime Minister
Republic of India

(Signed) **Zulfikar Ali Bhutto**

President
Islamic Republic of Pakistan

*Shimla, the 2nd July 1972*

# Appendix D: The Lahore Declaration

### The Lahore Declaration
### February 21, 1999

The Prime Ministers of the Republic of India and the Islamic Republic of Pakistan:-

*Sharing* a vision of peace and stability between their countries, and of progress and prosperity for their peoples;

*Convinced* that durable peace and development of harmonious relations and friendly cooperation will serve the vital interests of the peoples of the two countries, enabling them to devote their energies for a better future;

*Recognizing* that the nuclear dimension of the security environment of the two countries adds to their responsibility for avoidance of conflict between the two countries;

*Committed* to the principles and purposes of the Charter of the United Nations, and the universally accepted principles of peaceful co- existence;

*Reiterating* the determination of both countries to implementing the Shimla Agreement in letter and spirit;

*Committed* to the objective of universal nuclear disarmament and non-proliferation;

*Convinced* of the importance of mutually agreed confidence building measures for improving the security environment;

*Recalling* their agreement of 23rd September, 1998, that an environment of peace and security is in the supreme national interest of both sides and that the resolution of all outstanding issues, including Jammu and Kashmir, is essential for this purpose;

Have agreed that their respective Governments:-

Shall intensify their efforts to resolve all issues, including the issue of Jammu and Kashmir.

Shall refrain from intervention and interference in each other's internal affairs.

Shall intensify their composite and integrated dialogue process for an early and positive outcome of the agreed bilateral agenda.

Shall take immediate steps for reducing the risk of accidental or unauthorized use of nuclear weapons and discuss concepts and doctrines with a view to elaborating measures for confidence building in the nuclear and conventional fields, aimed at prevention of conflict.

Reaffirm their commitment to the goals and objectives of SAARC and to concert their efforts towards the realization of the SAARC vision for the year 2000 and beyond with a view to promoting the welfare of the peoples of South Asia and to improve their quality of life through accelerated economic growth, social progress and cultural development.

Reaffirm their condemnation of terrorism in all its forms and manifestations and their determination to combat this menace.

Shall promote and protect all human rights and fundamental freedoms.

Signed at Lahore on the 21st day of February 1999.

Atal Behari Vajpayee

Prime Minister of the Republic of India

Muhammad Nawaz Sharif

Prime Minister of the Islamic Republic of Pakistan

## MEMORANDUM OF UNDERSTANDING

The following is the text of the Memorandum of Understanding signed by the Foreign Secretary, Mr. K. Raghunath, and the Pakistan Foreign Secretary, Mr. Shamshad Ahmad, in Lahore on Sunday:

The Foreign Secretaries of India and Pakistan:-

Reaffirming the continued commitment of their respective governments to the principles and purposes of the U.N. Charter; Reiterating the determination of both countries to implementing the Shimla Agreement in letter and spirit; Guided by the agreement between their Prime Ministers of 23 September 1998 that an environment of peace and security is in the supreme national interest of both sides and that resolution of all outstanding issues, including Jammu and Kashmir, is essential for this purpose; Pursuant to the directive given by their respective Prime Ministers in Lahore, to adopt measures for promoting a stable environment of peace, and security between the two countries; Have on this day, agreed to the following:-

1. The two sides shall engage in bilateral consultations on security concepts, and nuclear doctrines, with a view to developing measures for confidence building in the nuclear and conventional fields, aimed at avoidance of conflict.

2. The two sides undertake to provide each other with advance notification in respect of ballistic missile flight tests, and shall conclude a bilateral agreement in this regard.

3. The two sides are fully committed to undertaking national measures to reducing the risks of accidental or unauthorized use of nuclear weapons under their respective control. The two sides further undertake to notify each, other immediately in the event of any accidental, unauthorized or unexplained incident that could create the risk of a fallout with adverse consequences for both sides, or an outbreak of a nuclear war between the two countries, as well as to adopt measures aimed at diminishing the possibility of such actions, or such incidents being misinterpreted by the other. The two sides shall identify/establish the appropriate communication mechanism for this purpose.

4. The two sides shall continue to abide by their respective unilateral moratorium on conducting further nuclear test explosions unless either side, in exercise of its national sovereignty decides that extraordinary events have jeopardized its supreme interests.

5. The two sides shall conclude an agreement on prevention of incidents at sea in order to ensure safety of navigation by naval vessels, and aircraft belonging to the two sides.
6. The two sides shall periodically review the implementation of existing Confidence Building Measures (CBMs) and where necessary, set up appropriate consultative mechanisms to monitor and ensure effective implementation of these CBMs.
7. The two sides shall undertake a review of the existing communication links (e.g. between the respective Directors-General, Military Operations) with a view to upgrading and improving these links, and to provide for fail-safe and secure communications.
8. The two sides shall engage in bilateral consultations on security, disarmament and non-proliferation issues within the context of negotiations on these issues in multilateral fora.

Where required, the technical details of the above measures will be worked out by experts of the two sides in meetings to be held on mutually agreed dates, before mid 1999 with a view to reaching bilateral agreements.

Done at Lahore on 21st February 1999 in the presence of Prime Minister of India, Mr. Atal Behari Vajpayee, and Prime Minister of Pakistan, Mr. Muhammad Nawaz Sharif.

(K. Raghunath)
*Foreign Secretary of the Republic of India*
(Shamshad Ahmad)
*Foreign Secretary of the Islamic Republic of Pakistan*

# Appendix E: The India–Pakistan Non-Attack Agreement

India–Pakistan Non-Attack Agreement
Agreement between India and Pakistan on the Prohibition of Attack against Nuclear Installations and Facilities
December 31, 1988

The Government of the Islamic Republic of Pakistan and the Government of the Republic of India, herein after referred to as the Contracting Parties, reaffirming their commitment to durable peace and the development of friendly and harmonious bilateral relations; conscious of the role of confidence building measures in promoting such bilateral relations based on mutual trust and goodwill; have agreed as follows:

1.

   i. Each party shall refrain from undertaking, encouraging or participating in, directly or indirectly, any action aimed at causing the destruction of, or damage to, any nuclear installation or facility in the other country.

   ii. The term "nuclear installation or facility" includes nuclear power and research reactors, fuel fabrication, uranium enrichment, isotopes separation and reprocessing facilities as well as any other installations with fresh or irradiated nuclear fuel and materials in any form and establishments storing significant quantities of radio-active materials.

2. Each Contracting Party shall inform the other on 1st January of each calendar year of the latitude and longitude of its nuclear installations and facilities and whenever there is any change.
3. This Agreement is subject to ratification. It shall come into force with effect from the date on which the Instruments of Ratification are exchanged.

Done at Islamabad on this Thirty-first day of December 1988, in, two copies each in Urdu, Hindi and English, the English text being authentic in case of any difference or dispute of interpretation.
[Signed:]

**Humayun Khan**

Foreign Secretary

*Islamic Republic of Pakistan*
**K.P.S. Menon**

Foreign Secretary

*Republic of India*
*Instruments of Ratification Exchanged: December 1990 (Entry into Force)*

# Appendix F: Charts, data and calculations by Jack Renner

*Sources*: World Bank, Index Mundi, CIA World Factbook, and Trading Economics

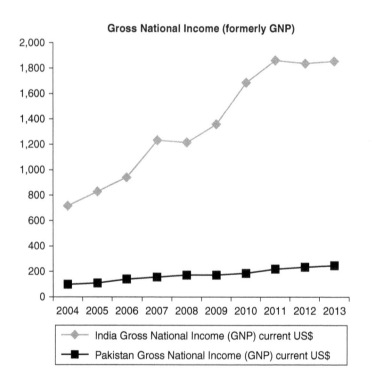

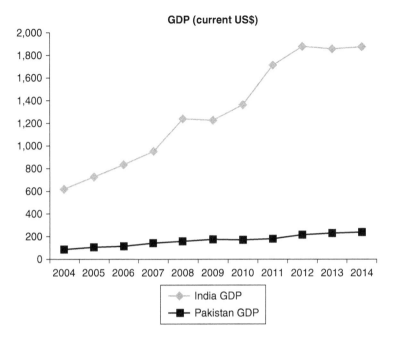

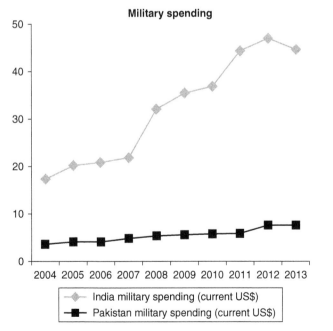

*Appendix F*

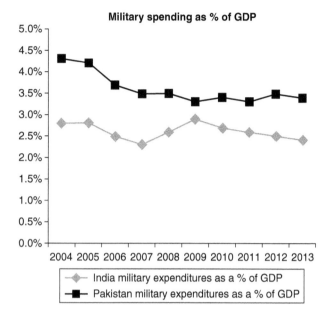

**Military spending as % of GDP**

India military expenditures as a % of GDP

Pakistan military expenditures as a % of GDP

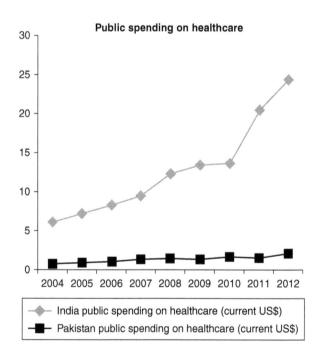

**Public spending on healthcare**

India public spending on healthcare (current US$)

Pakistan public spending on healthcare (current US$)

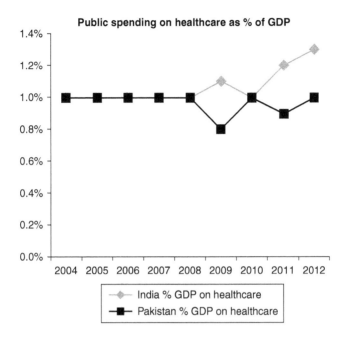

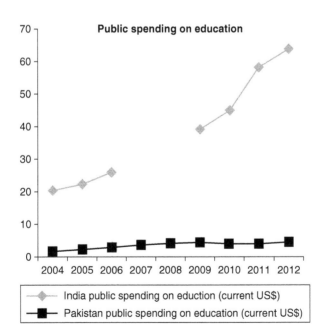

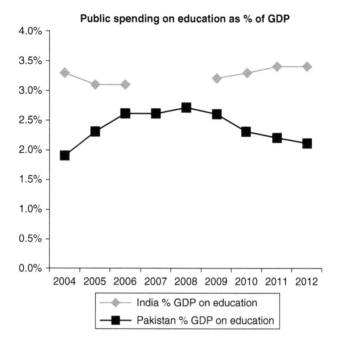

**Public spending on education as % of GDP**

Legend:
— India % GDP on education
— Pakistan % GDP on education

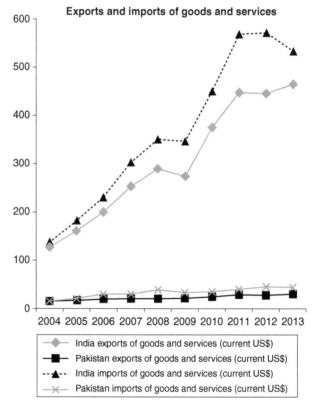

**Exports and imports of goods and services**

Legend:
— India exports of goods and services (current US$)
— Pakistan exports of goods and services (current US$)
--▲-- India imports of goods and services (current US$)
—×— Pakistan imports of goods and services (current US$)

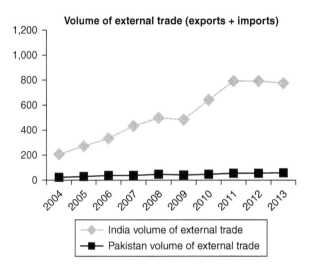

# Appendix G: Maps

## Siachen Glacier

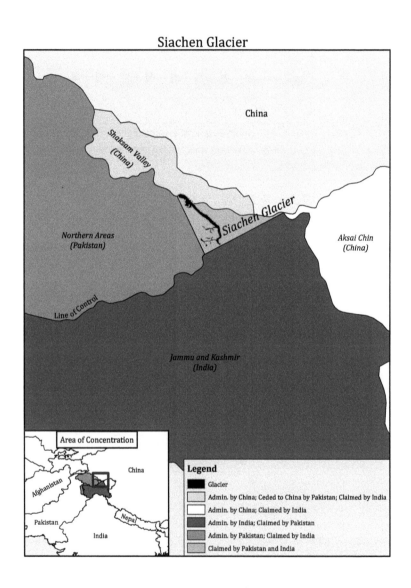

# Contested territories

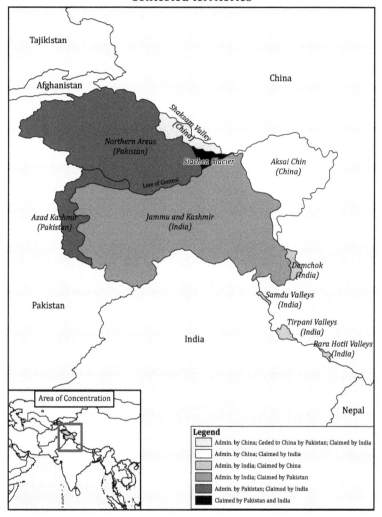

Tajikistan

Afghanistan

China

Shaksam Valley
(China)

Northern Areas
(Pakistan)

Siachen Glacier

Aksai Chin
(China)

Line of Control

Azad Kashmir
(Pakistan)

Jammu and Kashmir
(India)

Damchok
(India)

Samdu Valleys
(India)

Pakistan

Tirpani Valleys
(India)

Bara Hotii Valleys
(India)

India

Nepal

Area of Concentration

**Legend**
Admin. by China; Ceded to China by Pakistan; Claimed by India
Admin. by China; Claimed by India
Admin. by India; Claimed by China
Admin. by India; Claimed by Pakistan
Admin. by Pakistan; Claimed by India
Claimed by Pakistan and India

# REFERENCES

BOOKS

Advani, L.K. *My Country, My Life*. New Delhi: Rupa & Company, 2010.

Ali, Chaudhry Mohammed. *The Emergence of Pakistan*. Lahore: Research Society of Pakistan, 1983.

Asia Watch and Physicians for Human Rights. *The Human Rights Crisis in Kashmir: A Pattern of Impunity*. New York: Human Rights Watch, 1993.

Austin, Granville. *The Indian Constitution: Cornerstone of a Nation*. New Delhi: Oxford University Press, 1999.

Bajpai, Kanti, Afsir Karim and Amitabh Mattoo, eds. *Kargil and After: Challenges for Indian Policy*. New Delhi: Har-Anand, 2001.

Bajpai, Kanti, P.R. Chari, Pervaiz Iqbal Cheema, Stephen P. Cohen and Sumit Ganguly. *Brasstacks and Beyond: Perception and the Management of Crisis in South Asia*. New Delhi: Manohar Books, 1995.

Bammi, Lieutenant-General Y.M. *Kargil: The Impregnable Conquered*. Noida: Gorkha Publishers, 2002.

Bass, Gary J. *The Blood Telegram: Nixon, Kissinger and a Forgotten Genocide*. New York: Alfred A. Knopf, 2013.

Behera, Navnita Chadha. *Demystifying Kashmir*. Washington, DC: The Brookings Institution, 2006.

Bhargava, G.S. *South Asian Security after Afghanistan*. Lexington: D.C. Heath and Company, 1983.

Booth, Ken and Nicholas J. Wheeler, eds. *The Security Dilemma: Fear, Cooperation and Trust in World Politics*. London: Palgrave Macmillan, 2007.

Brass, Paul R. *Language, Religion and Politics in North India*. Cambridge: Cambridge University Press, 1974.

Brines, Russell. *The Indo-Pakistani Conflict*. New York: Pall Mall, 1968.

Burke, S.M. *Mainsprings of Indian and Pakistani Foreign Policies*. Lahore: Oxford University Press, 1975.

Chari, P.R. and Pervaiz Iqbal Cheema. *The Simla Agreement 1972: Its Wasted Promise*. New Delhi: Manohar Books, 2001.

Chari, P.R., Pervaiz Iqbal Cheema and Stephen P. Cohen. *Four Crises and a Peace Process: American Engagement in South Asia*. Washington, DC: Brookings, 2007.

*Perception, Politics and Security in South Asia: The Compound Crisis of 1990*. London: RoutledgeCurzon, 2003.

Chaudhuri, Rudra. *Forged in Crisis: India and the United States Since 1947*. London: Christopher Hurst and Company, 2014.

Chester, Lucy P. *Borders and Conflict in South Asia: The Radcliffe Boundary Commission and the Partition of the Punjab*. Manchester: Manchester University Press, 2009.

Chopra, Pran Nath. *India's Second Liberation*. Cambridge, MA: MIT Press, 1974.

Chowdhury, Srinjoy. *Despatches from Kargil*. New Delhi: Penguin Books, 2000.

Clarke, Ryan. *Lashkar-I-Taiba: The Fallacy of Subservient Proxies and the Future of Islamist Terrorism in India*. Carlisle Barracks: United States Army War College, 2010.

Cohen, Stephen P. and Sunil Dasgupta. *Arming Without Aiming: India's Military Modernization*. Washington, DC: The Brookings Institution, 2010.

Dasgupta, Chandrasekhar. *War and Diplomacy in Kashmir, 1947–1948*. New Delhi: Sage, 2002.

Datta-Ray, Sunanda K. *Smash and Grab: Annexation of Sikkim*. Delhi: Westland, 1984.

Dixit, J.N. *India-Pakistan in War and Peace*. New Delhi: Books Today, 2002.

Dossani, Rafiq and Henry S. Rowen, eds. *Prospects for Peace in South Asia*. Stanford: Stanford University Press, 2005.

Fair, C. Christine. *Fighting to the End: The Pakistan Army's Way of War*. New York: Oxford University Press, 2014.

*India and Pakistan Engagement: Prospects for Breakthrough or Breakdown*, Special Report 129, January 2005. Washington, DC: United States Institute of Peace, 2005.

Gall, Carlotta. *The Wrong Enemy: America in Afghanistan, 2001–2014*. New York: Houghton Mifflin, 2014.

Ganguly, Sumit. *Conflict Unending: India-Pakistan Tensions Since 1947*. New York: Columbia University Press, 2001.

*The Crisis in Kashmir: Portents of War, Hopes of Peace.* New York: Cambridge University Press, 1997.

*India's Role in Afghanistan.* Barcelona: CIDOB, 2012.

Ganguly, Sumit and David P. Fidler, eds. *India and Counterinsurgency: Lessons Learned.* London: Routledge, 2009.

Ganguly, Sumit and Devin Hagerty. *Fearful Symmetry: India-Pakistan Crises Under the Shadow of Nuclear Weapons.* Seattle: University of Washington Press, 2006.

Ganguly, Sumit and S. Paul Kapur. *India, Pakistan and the Bomb: Debating Nuclear Stability in South Asia.* New York: Columbia University Press, 2010.

Glaser, Charles L. *Rational Theory of International Politics: The Logic of Competition and Cooperation.* Princeton: Princeton University Press, 2010.

Goodson, Larry. *Afghanistan's Endless War: State Failure, Regional Politics and the Rise of the Taliban.* Seattle: University of Washington Press, 2001.

Guha, Ramachandra. *India After Gandhi: The History of the World's Largest Democracy.* New York: Ecco, 2007.

Gupta, Jyoti Bhusan Das. *Indo-Pakistan Relations, 1947–1955.* Amsterdam: De Brug Djambatan, 1958.

*Jammu and Kashmir.* The Hague: Martinus Nijhoff, 1968.

Gupta, Sisir. *Kashmir: A Study in India-Pakistan Relations.* New Delhi: Asia Publishing House, 1967.

Hanauer, Larry and Peter Chalk. *India's and Pakistan's Strategies in Afghanistan: Implications for the US and the Region.* Santa Monica: Rand Corporation, 2012.

Hart, Henry, ed. *Indira Gandhi's India: A Political System Reappraised.* Boulder: Westview, 1976.

Hodson, H.V. *The Great Divide: Britain, India and Pakistan.* New York: Random House, 1969.

Howenstein, Nicholas. *The Jihadi Terrain in Pakistan: An Introduction to the Sunni Jihadi Groups in Pakistan and Kashmir.* Bradford: University of Bradford, Pakistan Security Research Unit, 2008.

Hussain, Zahid. *Frontline Pakistan: The Struggle With Militant Islam.* New York: Columbia University Press, 2007.

Hyder, Mohammed. *October Coup: A Memoir of the Struggle for Hyderabad.* New Delhi: Roli Books, 2012.

Hyman, Anthony, Muhammed Ghayur and Naresh Kaushik. *Pakistan: Zia and After ....* New Delhi: Abhinav Publishers, 1989.

Jackson, Robert. *South Asian Crisis: India, Pakistan, Bangla Desh.* London: Chatto & Windus, 1975.

Jahan, Rounaq. *Pakistan: Failure in National Integration.* New York: Columbia University Press, 1972.

Jalal, Ayesha. *The Struggle for Pakistan: A Muslim Homeland and Global Politics.* Cambridge, MA: Harvard University Press, 2014.

Jamal, Arif. *Call For Transnational Jihad: Lashkar-e-Taiba, 1985–2014.* Portland: Avantgarde Books, 2014.

*Shadow War: The Untold Story of Jihad in Kashmir.* New York: Melville House, 2009.

Jervis, Robert. *Perception and Misperception in International Politics.* Princeton: Princeton University Press, 1976.

Jervis, Robert, Richard Ned Lebow and Janice Gross Stein. *Psychology and Deterrence.* Baltimore: Johns Hopkins University Press, 1985.

Jha, Prem Shankar. *Kashmir 1947: Rival Versions of History.* New Delhi: Oxford University Press, 2003.

Jones, Owen Bennett. *Pakistan: Eye of the Storm.* New Haven: Yale University Press, 2002.

Jones, Seth G. *In the Graveyard of Empires: America's War in Afghanistan.* New York: W.W. Norton and Company, 2010.

Kapadia, Harish. *Siachen Glacier: The Battle of Roses.* New Delhi: Rupa, 2010.

Kapur, S. Paul. *Dangerous Deterrent: Nuclear Weapons Proliferation and Conflict in South Asia.* Stanford: Stanford University Press, 2007.

Khan, Akbar. *Raiders in Kashmir.* Lahore: National Book Foundation, 1975.

Khan, Asghar. *The First Round: Indo-Pakistan War 1965.* New Delhi: Vikas, 1979.

Krishna, Major-General Ashok and P.R. Chari, eds. *Kargil: The Tables Turned.* New Delhi: Manohar, 2001.

Kydd, Andrew H. *Trust and Mistrust in International Relations.* Princeton: Princeton University Press, 2005.

Lamb, Alastair. *Kashmir: A Disputed Legacy.* Hertingfordbury: Roxford Books, 1991.

Lambeth, Benjamin S. *Airpower at 18,000 Feet: The Indian Air Force in the Kargil War.* Washington, DC: Carnegie Endowment for International Peace, 2012.

Lavoy, Peter, ed. *Asymmetric Warfare in South Asia.* New York: Cambridge University Press, 2009.

Levy, Adrian and Cathy Scott-Clark. *The Meadow: Kashmir 1995 – Where the Terror Began.* London: HarperPress, 2012.

Low, D.A., ed. *The Political Inheritance of Pakistan*. New York: St. Martin's Press, 1991.

Lustick, Ian S. *Unsettled States, Disputed Lands: Britain and Ireland, France and Algeria, Israel and the West Bank-Gaza*. Ithaca: Cornell University Press, 1995.

Malik, General V.P. *Kargil: From Surprise to Victory*. New Delhi: HarperCollins, 2006.

Malik, Hafeez. *Muslim Nationalism in India and Pakistan*. Washington, DC: Public Affairs Press, 1963.

McGrath, Allen. *The Destruction of Pakistan's Democracy*. Karachi: Oxford University Press, 1996.

Mearsheimer, John. *Conventional Deterrence*. Ithaca: Cornell University Press, 1983.

Menon, V.P. *The Transfer of Power in India*. New Delhi: Orient Blackswan, 1997.

Misra, K.P., ed. *Janata's Foreign Policy*. New Delhi: Vikas Publishing House, 1979.

Musharraf, Pervez. *In the Line of Fire: A Memoir*. New York: Free Press, 2006.

Narang, Vipin. *Nuclear Strategy in the Modern Era: Regional Powers and International Conflict*. Princeton: Princeton University Press, 2014.

Nehru, Jawaharlal. *The Discovery of India*. New Delhi: Oxford University Press, 1994.

Padder, Sajad. *The Composite Dialogue between India and Pakistan: Structure, Process and Agency*, Working Paper No. 65, *Heidelberg Papers in South Asian and Comparative Politics*. Heidelberg: South Asia Institute, Heidelberg University, 2012.

Palit, Major-General D.K. *War in the High Himalaya: The Indian Army in Crisis*. London: C. Hurst and Company, 1991.

Paul, T.V., ed. *The Indo-Pakistani Conflict: An Enduring Rivalry*. New York: Cambridge University Press, 2006.

Paul, T.V. *The Warrior State: Pakistan in the Contemporary World*. New York: Oxford University Press, 2014.

Prime Minister's High Level Committee. *Social, Economic and Educational Status of the Muslim Community in India*. New Delhi: Department of Minority Affairs, 2006.

Raghavan, Lieutenant-General V.R. *Siachen: Conflict Without End*. New Delhi: Viking, 2002.

Raghavan, Srinath. *1971: A Global History of the Creation of Bangladesh*. Cambridge, MA: Harvard University Press, 2013.

Rashid, Ahmed. *Taliban: Militant Islam, Oil and Fundamentalism in Central Asia*. New Haven: Yale University Press, 2001.

Rasler, Karen, William R. Thompson and Sumit Ganguly. *How Rivalries End*. Philadelphia: University of Pennsylvania Press, 2013.

Reidel, Bruce. *American Diplomacy and the 1999 Kargil Summit at Blair House*. Philadelphia: University of Pennsylvania Press, 2002.

  *Deadly Embrace: Pakistan, America and the Future of the Global Jihad*. Washington, DC: Brookings, 2011.

Rose, Leo E. and Richard Sisson. *War and Secession: Pakistan, India, and the Creation of Bangladesh*. Oakland: University of California Press, 1991.

Rubinoff, Arthur G. *India's Use of Force in Goa*. Bombay: Popular Prakashan, 1971.

Sattar, Abdul. *Case Study on Comparisons of Lahore, Agra and Islamabad Summits*. Lahore: Pakistan Institute of Legislative Development and Transparency, 2004.

Sayeed, Khalid bin. *Pakistan: The Formative Phase, 1947–1948*. Karachi: Pakistan Publishing House, 1960.

Schaffer, Howard B. and Teresita C. Schaffer. *How Pakistan Negotiates with the United States: Riding the Roller Coaster*. Washington, DC: The United States Institute of Peace, 2011.

Sen, Lionel Protip. *Slender Was the Thread*. New Delhi: Orient Longmans, 1969.

Shah, Aqil. *The Army and Democracy: Military Politics in Pakistan*. Cambridge, MA: Harvard University Press, 2014

Singh, Amarinder. *A Ridge Too Far: War in the Kargil Heights 1999*. Patiala: Moti Bagh Palace, 2001.

Singh, Gurharpal. *Ethnic Conflict in India: A Case Study of Punjab*. New York: Palgrave Macmillan, 2000.

Singh, Jasjit, ed. *Kargil 1999: Pakistan's Fourth War for Kashmir*. New Delhi: Knowledge World, 1999.

Singh, Jaswant. *A Call to Honour: In Service of Emergent India*. New Delhi: Rupa and Company, 2006.

Sood, Let. Gen. V.K. and Pravin Sawhney. *Operation Parakram: The War Unfinished*. New Delhi: Sage Publications, 2003.

Stolar, Alex. *To The Brink: Indian Decision-Making and the 2001–2002 Standoff*. Washington, DC: The Henry L. Stimson Center, 2008.

Swami, Praveen. *India, Pakistan and the Secret Jihad: The Covert War in Kashmir, 1947–2004*. London: Routledge, 2007.

  *The Kargil War*. New Delhi: LeftWord Books, 2000.

Talbott, Strobe. *Democracy, Diplomacy and the Bomb*. Washington, DC: The Brookings Institution, 2006.

Talbott, Strobe. *Engaging India: Diplomacy, Democracy and the Bomb*. Washington, DC: The Brookings Institution, 2004.

Tang, Shiping. *A Theory of Security Strategy for Our Time: Defensive Realism*. New York: Palgrave Macmillan, 2010.

Tarapore, Arzan. *Holocaust or Hollow Victory: Limited War in Nuclear South Asia*. New Delhi: Institute of Peace and Conflict Studies, 2006.

Tellis, Ashley J., C. Christine Fair and Jamison Jo Medby. *Limited Conflicts Under the Nuclear Umbrella: Indian and Pakistani Lessons from the Kashmir Crisis*. Santa Monica: RAND Corporation, 2001.

Tudor, Maya. *The Promise of Power: The Origins of Authoritarianism in Pakistan and Democracy in India*. Cambridge: Cambridge University Press, 2013.

Verma, Major-General Ashok Kalyan. *Blood on the Snow: Tactical Victory and Strategic Failure*. New Delhi: Manohar Books, 2002.

Vertzberger, Yaacov Y.I. *The World in Their Minds: Information Processing, Cognition, and Perception in Foreign Policy Decisionmaking*. Palo Alto: Stanford University Press, 1990.

Weaver, Mary Anne. *Pakistan: In the Shadow of Jihad and Afghanistan*. New York: Farrar, Straus and Giroux, 2002.

Whitehead, Andrew. *A Mission in Kashmir*. New York: Penguin, 2008.

Wilkinson, Steven I. *Army and Nation: The Military and Indian Democracy Since Independence*. Cambridge, MA: Harvard University Press, 2015.

Wirsing, Robert G. *Kashmir in the Shadow of War: Regional Rivalries in a Nuclear Age*. Armonk: M.E. Sharpe, 2003.

Yousaf, Mohammed and Mark Adkin. *The Bear Trap: Afghanistan's Untold Story*. Havetown: Casemate, 2001.

Yusuf, Moeed, ed. *Insurgency and Counterinsurgency in South Asia*. Washington, DC: United States Institute of Peace, 2014.

Zaheer, Hasan. *The Rawalpindi Conspiracy 1951: The First Coup Attempt in Pakistan*. Karachi: Oxford University Press, 1998.

   *The Rise and Realization of Bengali Muslim Nationalism*. New York: Oxford University Press, 1997.

### ARTICLES

Acosta, Marcus P. "The Kargil Conflict: Waging War in the Himalayas." *Small Wars and Insurgencies* 18, no. 3 (September 2007): 397–415.

Ahmed, Samina. "Pakistan's Nuclear Weapons Program: Turning Points and Nuclear Choices." *International Security* 23, no. 4 (Spring 1999): 178–204.

Ashraf, Air Commodore Tariq M. "Doctrinal Reawakening of the Indian Armed Forces." *Military Review* (November–December 2004): 53–62.

Asif, Bushra and Sean Farrell, "India-Pakistan: Breaking the Deadlock." *South Asia Monitor* (Washington, DC: South Asia Program Center for Strategic and International Studies), February 1, 2004.

Bajpai, Kanti. "Foreign Policy in 2001: What's Going On?" *Seminar*, Annual Issue, 2001.

Barton, Sir William. "Pakistan's Claim to Kashmir." *Foreign Affairs* 28 (January 1950): 279–308.

Basrur, Rajesh M. "Kargil, Terrorism, and India's Strategic Shift." *India Review* 1, no. 4 (October 2002): 39–56.

Bhola, P.L. "Indo-Pakistan Control March Over Siachen Glacier." *Indian Journal of Asian Affairs* 1, no. 1 (Summer 1988): 28–48.

Bommakanti, Kartik. "Coercion and Control: Explaining India's Victory at Kargil." *India Review* 10, no. 3 (2011): 283–328.

Bratton, Patrick. "Signals and Orchestration: India's Use of Compellence in the 2001–02 Crisis." *Strategic Analysis* 34, no. 4 (July 2010): 594–610.

Fair, C. Christine and Sumit Ganguly. "Lives on the Line." *The Washington Quarterly* 36, no. 3 (Summer 2013): 173–184.

Fearon, James D. "Rationalist Explanations for War." *International Organization* 49, no. 3 (Summer 1995): 379–414.

Ganguly, Sumit. "From the Defense of the Nation to Aid to the Civil: The Army in Contemporary India." *Journal of Asian and African Affairs* 26 (1991): 1–12.

"Deterrence Failure Revisited: The Indo-Pakistani Conflict of 1965." *Journal of Strategic Studies* 13, no. 4 (December 1990): 77–93.

"India's Pathway to Pokhran II: The Sources and Prospects of India's Nuclear Weapons Program." *International Security* 23, no. 4 (Spring 1999): 148–177.

"Will Kashmir Stop India's Rise?" *Foreign Affairs* 85, no. 4 (July/August 2006): 45–57.

"Pakistan's Never-Ending Story: Why the October Coup Was No Surprise." *Foreign Affairs* 79, no. 2 (March/April 2000): 2–9.

"War, Nuclear Weapons and Crisis Stability in South Asia." *Security Studies* 17, no. 1 (2008): 164–184.

Ganguly, Sumit and Michael R. Kraig. "The 2001–2002 Indo-Pakistani Crisis: Exposing the Limits of Coercive Diplomacy in South Asia." *Security Studies* 14, no. 2 (April–June 2005): 290–324.

Ganguly, Sumit and R. Harrison Wagner. "India and Pakistan: Bargaining in the Shadow of Nuclear War." *The Journal of Strategic Studies* 27, no. 3 (September 2004): 479–507.

Glaser, Charles L. "Why Even Good Defenses May be Bad." *International Security* 9, no. 2 (Fall 1984): 92–123.

Hagerty, Devin T. "Nuclear Deterrence in South Asia: The 1990 Indo-Pakistani Crisis." *International Security* 20, no. 3 (Winter 1995): 79–114.

Herz, John H. "Idealist Internationalism and the Security Dilemma." *World Politics* 2, no. 2 (January 1950): 157–180.

Howenstein, Nicholas and Sumit Ganguly, "India-Pakistan Rivalry in Afghanistan." *Journal of International Affairs* 63, no. 1 (Fall/Winter 2009): 127–140.

Ilahi, Shereen. "The Radcliffe Boundary Commission and the Fate of Kashmir." *India Review* 2, no. 1 (January 2003): 77–102.

Jervis, Robert. "Cooperation Under the Security Dilemma." *World Politics* 30, no. 2 (January 1976): 167–214.

"Dilemmas about Security Dilemmas." *Security Studies* 20, no. 3 (July–September 2011): 416–489.

Jones, Owen Bennett. "Musharraf's Kashmir Policy." *Asian Affairs* 38, no. III (November 2007): 305–317.

Joshi, Shashank "India's Military Instrument: A Doctrine Still Born." *Journal of Strategic Studies* 36, no. 4 (2013): 512–540.

Kalyanaraman, S. "Operation Parakram: An Indian Exercise in Coercive Diplomacy." *Strategic Analysis* 26, no. 4 (2002): 478–492.

Kapur, S. Paul. "India and Pakistan's Unstable Peace: Why Nuclear South Asia is Not Like Cold War Europe." *International Security* 30, no. 2 (Fall 2005): 127–152.

Kennedy, Andrew. "India's Nuclear Odyssey: Implicit Umbrellas, Diplomatic Disappointments and the Bomb." *International Security* 36, no. 2 (Fall 2011): 120–153.

Khan, Aarish U. "Siachen Glacier: Getting Past the Deadlock." *Spotlight on Regional Affairs* 31, no. 5 (May 2012): 1–25.

Ladwig III, Walter C. "A Cold Start to Hot Wars? The Indian Army's New Limited War Doctrine." *International Security* 32, no. 3 (Winter 2007/8): 158–190.

"Indian Military Modernization and Conventional Deterrence in South Asia." *Journal of Strategic Studies* (May 2015): 1–4.

Narang, Vipin. "Posturing for Peace? Pakistan's Nuclear Postures and South Asian Security." *International Security* 34, no. 3 (Winter 2009/10): 38–78.

Nasr, Vali Reza. "Military Rule, Islamism and Democracy in Pakistan." *Middle East Journal* 58, no. 2 (Spring 2004): 195–209.

Noorani, A.G. "Search for New Relationships in the Indian Subcontinent." *The World Today* 31, no. 6 (June 1975): 240–248.

O'Ballance, Edgar. "The 1965 War in Retrospect." *Defence Journal* 7 (1978): 15–19.

Pardesi, Manjeet S. "Is India a Great Power? Understanding Great Power Status in Contemporary International Relations." *Asian Security* 11, no. 1 (2015): 1–30.

Qadir, Shaukat. "An Analysis of the Kargil Conflict 1999." *Journal of the Royal United Services Institution* 147, no. 2 (April 2002): 24–30.

Quinlan, Phillip J. "Pakistan: A Conflicted Ally in the Fight Against Terrorism Since 9/11." *Global Security Studies* 3, no. 1 (Winter 2012): 1–14.

Raghavan, Srinath. "Soldiers, Statesmen, and India's Security Policy." *India Review* 11, no. 2 (April–June 2012): 116–133.

Rahgavan, V.R. "Limited War and Nuclear Escalation in South Asia." *The Nonproliferation Review* 8, no. 3 (Fall/Winter 2001): 1–18.

Rizvi, Hasan-Askari. "Civil-Military Relations in Contemporary Pakistan." *Survival* 40, no. 2 (1998): 96–113.

Schweller, Randall L. "Neorealism's Status-Quo Bias: What Security Dilemma?" *Security Studies* 5, no. 3 (1996): 90–121.

Singh, Bhartendu Kumar. "Chinese Views on the Kargil Conflict." *Institute of Peace and Conflict Studies*, New Delhi, June 25, 1999.

Singh, S. Nihal. "Why India Goes to Moscow for Arms." *Asian Survey* 24, no. 7 (July 1984): 707–740.

Smith, Jeff M. "Sino-Indian Relations: A Troubled History, An Uncertain Future." *Harvard International Review* 33, no. 1 (Spring 2011).

Sukumaran, R. "The 1962 India-China War and Kargil 1999: Restrictions on the Use of Air Power." *Strategic Analysis* 27, no. 3 (July–September 2003): 332–355.

Talbot, Ian. "Pakistan in 2002: Democracy, Terrorism, and Brinkmanship." *Asian Survey* 43, no. 1 (January/February 2003): 198–207.

Tang, Shiping. "The Security Dilemma: A Conceptual Analysis." *Security Studies* 18, no. 3 (2009): 587–623.

Telford, Hamish. "Counter-Insurgency in India: Observations from Punjab and Kashmir." *The Journal of Conflict Studies* 21, no. 1 (2001): 1–27.

Wheeler, Nicholas J. "'I Had Gone to Lahore With a Message of Goodwill But in Return We Got Kargil': The Promise and Perils of 'Leaps of Trust' in India-Pakistan Relations." *India Review* 9, no. 3 (July–September 2010): 319–344.

Wirsing, Robert. "The Siachen Glacier Dispute: The Strategic Dimension." *Strategic Studies* 12 (Autumn 1988): 38–54.

Zain, Omer Farooq. "Siachen Glacier Conflict: Discordant in Pakistan-India Reconciliation." *Pakistan Horizon* 59, no. 2 (April 2006): 73–82.

# INDEX

For EU product safety concerns, contact us at Calle de José Abascal, 56–1°, 28003 Madrid, Spain or eugpsr@cambridge.org.

www.ingramcontent.com/pod-product-compliance
Ingram Content Group UK Ltd.
Pitfield, Milton Keynes, MK11 3LW, UK
UKHW020324140625
459647UK00018B/2001